What Makes People Tick?

By the same author:
Love Coach
Body Language Secrets

What Makes People Tick?

The Ultimate Guide to Personality Types

Susan Quilliam

Element
An Imprint of HarperCollins*Publishers*
77–85 Fulham Palace Road
Hammersmith, London W6 8JB

The website address is: www.thorsonselement.com

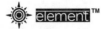

and *Element* are trademarks of
HarperCollins*Publishers* Ltd

First published by Element 2003

10 9 8 7 6 5 4 3 2 1

© Susan Quilliam 2003

Cartoons by Harry Venning

Susan Quilliam asserts the moral right to
be identified as the author of this work

A catalogue record of this book
is available from the British Library

ISBN 0 7225 3990 8

Printed and bound in Great Britain by
Martins the Printers, Berwick upon Tweed

Contents

HOW PERSONALITY WORKS 4
Interaction patterns:

HOW PERSONALITY WORKS 5
Group patterns:

About the author

Susan Quilliam is a relationships psychologist and established author. She has written 16 books, published in 21 languages and 24 countries, including *Body Language Secrets*. Susan has written best-selling books with Relate and The Samaritans and is a columnist for a number of British and American magazines and websites, including *FHM*, *FHMUS* and *Good Housekeeping*.

Acknowledgements

This book has been a joy to write and a great deal of that joy is down to the people who have been involved.

So thanks to all my friends and colleagues whose stories have appeared in this book and who have helped test the quizzes, including Andy Wilson, Anna Dalton, Beckie Stones, Bhanu Halai, Christine G. N. Day, Clare Askew, Corinne Sweet, David Spacey, Emma Williams, Fin Shirlaw, Gladeana McMahon, Glenn Gentry, Hazel Lonergan, Ian Harley, Ingrid Statman, Irene Stockdale, Jacolyn Harmer, Jane Matthews, Jane Warren, Jill English, Kate Newman, Kate Williams, Katherine Cairns, Kitty Grove-Stephensen, Leo McNeir, Linda Kelly, Linda Newman, Liz Annetts, Loredana Harley, Lynne Singleton, Miles Foster, Mike Young, Miranda Broadhurst, Mo Shapiro, Nick Booth, Nicola Renson, Noeline Armstrong, Patsy Povey-Turner, Paul Newman, Phil Freeman, Richard Broome, Rob 'Stadium' Heels, Roger Dowling, Sandra Murphy, Sarah Ford, Sima Miller-Bridger, Simon Anscombe, Simon Collins, Sonia Nicholson, Sue Linge, Sue Ogle, Susanna Mendonca, Tom Whitehouse, Trevor Day and Val Glover.

Thanks, as always, to Barbara Levy, my agent, for her (so far) sixteen years of professional expertise and personal support.

Thanks too to everyone at Thorsons for commissioning, producing and backing this book, especially Wanda Whiteley, Paul Redhead, Susanna Abbott, Jo Lal, Meg Slyfield and Harry Venning.

Thanks to my assistants Linda Newman and Nicola Renson for their support, research and organization.

Finally, a special thank you to Michelle Woolley for her research, her editing – and for the hours of energy, effort and creative flexibility she put in to making sure the quizzes work!

All statistics in this book are taken from research done by Rodger Bailey on the Language and Behaviour Profile and from Tad James and Wyatt Woodsmall's book *Time Line Therapy and the Basis of Personality* (Meta Publications, 1998) to whom I offer my acknowledgements and gratitude.

To Ian, who as always makes all things possible.

About this book

What do you think when you look in the mirror every morning? Do you feel you know yourself inside out? Or do you sometimes wonder who you really are – why on earth you think, feel and react as you do?

And what do you experience when you interact with other people – friends, workmates, your partner? Do you fully understand them, all the time every time? Or do you sometimes wonder what really makes them tick – and why they're so different from you?

What Makes People Tick? answers these questions. It provides a guided tour of personality patterns, a tour of the wonderfully complicated jigsaw puzzle that forms the human character. *What Makes People Tick?* will help you ...

- **understand yourself and how you work**
- **understand others and how they work**
- **get along with people**
- **convince others of your point of view**
- **understand how human beings develop the personalities they do**
- **cope with difficult people in your life**
- **cope when you are in, or leading, a group**
- **change your own personality**
- **find the career that suits you**
- **win the job that suits you**
- **choose the right partner and create the happiest relationship**
- **fulfil your personal potential in life**

So what does the book contain? It's divided into four parts – the personality patterns themselves; sections on using the patterns in life; diagnostic quizzes; and occasional pages explaining how personality works.

This is how to use the book. The first 20 chapters cover the different personality patterns. Before reading each, you should first answer the quiz at the back of the book relating to that chapter. Otherwise you may decide that a particular personality pattern seems more relevant or more acceptable as a description of you, and then mysteriously find yourself answering the quiz in a way that gives you the personality you want!

Within each chapter you will find specific sections relating to how the particular personality pattern can be used in different contexts. These are highlighted by icons in the margin.

$ This section shows how the pattern is relevant to work.

♥   This section shows how the pattern is relevant to love.

!   This section shows how the pattern is relevant to social life.

❀   This section shows how the pattern is relevant to personal development.

👥   This section shows how the pattern is relevant to being in a group.

ABC   This section shows how the pattern developed.

If you have a particular issue you want *What Makes People Tick?* to help you with, the chapters at the back of the book pull together useful information for use in various life arenas; reading other people, changing yourself, learning, choosing a career, getting a job, making a relationship work.

One final thing. Remember that personality extremes are rare. You'll probably fall midway along the spectrum of most patterns – so you have a great deal in common with most people in the world – whether or not they are of your gender, your age group, your race or your culture.

But every personality is also unique. Everyone has a mix of different personality patterns, in different amounts, with a different balance. So there will never be anyone else in the world with the same personality as yours.

Therefore – to make the most of life – value your own personality, appreciate other people's personalities ... and be sure to capitalize on both the similarities and the differences between the two!

Basic fascinations:
McClelland's motivator modes

(1) So here's the most basic piece of the personality puzzle. What in the world fascinates us? What really motivates us? What gives purpose to our lives? We're not talking anything as specific as 'job' or 'kids' or 'hobby'. We're talking fundamentals, as identified by psychologist David McClelland in the 1940s. He named three compulsions in people's minds, three things that drive us on.

Our fascination may be to do with people – affiliation. It may be with success – achievement. It may be with being in charge – influence. These three motivators underpin every single part of human behaviour. Every one of us needs support and validation – needs the satisfaction of doing well, needs to be able to affect other people. So everyone has some of all three motivators.

Want to know your own motivator mode? See page 252.

Affiliators

If our main motivator is affiliation, we're fascinated by people. We value others enormously. We place the human race at the centre of our world.

So we may love people watching and people meeting – we not only sit at a street cafe watching the world go by, but catch people's eyes, get talking to them and end up exchanging Christmas cards for the next ten years. We may have a large network of contacts, kept going on a reciprocal deal of help and help alike – and we hate it when we argue or are cut off from friends.

The most affiliation-driven woman I know celebrated her

fiftieth birthday not only by inviting 250 of *her* closest friends to party, but getting them all to give a charity donation instead of a birthday present – so they helped other people too.

She's a social butterfly – but affiliators don't have to be an extrovert or even socially competent. We often prefer our contact one-on-one, have just a few close friends or may even be loners. The main issue here is that an affiliator thinks people are the most important thing, values them enormously, is affected by them deeply.

The colleague who told me that since she was thirteen her life's dream has been to die surrounded by her children, grandchildren and great-grand children is an affiliator. How could she be anything else?

Women tend to be affiliators: a 1990 study suggested that 70–80% of women see the family as their priority.

Achievers

Steve Jobs, founder of Apple Computers, once said he wanted to 'put a ding in the universe'. Spot the achiever! Because if we're driven by achievement, what's important is to 'get a result'.

By 'result' we might mean success in the day job – in which case, if we're a high level achiever, we'll happily work until four in the morning to get that deadline met. But we might just as well mean success in relationship – in which case, we'll want to have the most perfect love affair in the history of the universe, ever. Or we might have as our goal a more abstract life aim – like Steve Jobs, we may want to be the one who impresses, revolutionizes or even saves the world.

The key is that we want to get things done and dusted. If we succeed – whether that's in getting promotion or in getting the ironing done – the high we get is like nothing else in the world.

There can be a downside. Achievers are often workaholics, who take the mobile, pager and laptop on a beach holiday and don't

what makes people tick?

Affiliation.   Achievement.   Influence.

notice when their relationships go down the tubes. And although achievers aren't necessarily competitive – in fact we may be extremely cooperative if it gets the job done – we can end up being a bit ruthless on our scramble to the top.

That said, achievers have one big strength – we get results. Achievers work hard at jobs. Achievers take and pass exams. Above all, achievers strive to be good in whatever we do. The school report that commented 'Melanie must learn not to cry when she comes second' was written about an achiever.

Men tend to be achievers and influencers – the 1990 study suggested that 70-80% of men see work as their main priority.

Influencers

If we're motivated by influence, we're fascinated by power. In its purest form, we'll want power for its own sake – politicking, infighting, wheeling and dealing. The greatest dictators were all off-the-scale influencers.

More likely, we just want to know we're safe, in charge in our own world; we don't want to control people, we just want to know we can affect them.

We're not necessarily out to hurt – we may like to give people wonderful presents to see the look of surprise and pleasure on their face. One influencer I know came home buzzing after three days organizing a garden fête – a garden fête, for heaven's sake, hardly your ultimate power arena – because the people he'd pulled in favours from respected him enough to say yes.

And an influencer doesn't always actively want control. Sometimes he just likes to watch. One of the most influence-oriented people I've ever met is a political commentator who keeps a low profile, but is utterly fascinated by the in-fighting he sees around him. (He also compulsively does a postmortem on every party he attends, having unerringly spotted every looming divorce.)

As a society we're wary of influencers – we say 'power corrupts and absolute power corrupts absolutely'. And sometimes, of course, it does.

But influencing isn't bad in itself. We all need to have some effect over the people around us – if we don't have it, then we're slaves. And some form of hierarchy is necessary in society's wider scheme of things; we need leaders as well as followers, persuaders as well as persuadees, just in order to get things done.

The time to worry is if we don't want any influence – that means we've given up on ever being in control of our lives.

Cracking the combinations

It's vital to look at people's single 'key' motivators. But most people have a second motivator in a sufficient amount to affect the mix.

So combining affiliation and achievement gives a people-person who nevertheless gets the job done. If we've got this mixture, we're less likely to sit and natter than a pure affiliator, more likely to pass the paper hankies than a pure achiever. It's a typical and very effective combination – making for a strong manager at work, a focused family person at home.

Combining achievement and influence makes us a high-flyer, a go-getter, a tough negotiator. And if our motivations stay constant, then we're likely to get to the top and never look back. The only danger is that if later in life affiliation increases its importance to us, then we may glance back and wonder why our relationships went out the window years ago.

Affiliation and influence? A very unusual combination. And one that's likely to cause us – and our nearest and dearest – a lot of heartache. Because needing to be both close to people and have control over them can create clashes. We may sort it by meeting our affiliation needs when at home and our influence needs at work – resulting in the classic brute-force chairman who's a total teddy bear with family and friends.

But trouble will always be brewing as our people motivation makes us compromise our desire for influence – or our need for power alienates the people we most value in life.

The lowest subpattern

Finally, which motivator mode do we score lowest on? That's the one that will get us feeling envious – or threatened – if we see it in others, and very uncomfortable if we find it in ourselves.

So if we're low in affiliation, we may envy affiliators for their social competence. But we may see them as 'weak' or 'unfocused' – and if we find ourselves becoming more affiliation-oriented, we'll think we're losing our edge.

If we're very low in achievement, we'll see achievers as to be admired for their get up and go. But we may see them as hard and pushy – and if we ourselves start to push ahead and so become one of the dreaded high-flyers, we may backpedal or even deliberately sabotage ourselves.

If we have a very low influence motivation, we may feel intrigued by other people's power plays. But we may be outraged by it and – if we sense we're strongly influencing others – we may feel wary and end up consciously holding back.

In short, what we don't do defines our personality just as much as what we do do.

Getting together with

It's a self-evident truth that knowing someone's motivator mode will improve your relationship with them.

Friend, relative or colleague, if you appreciate their motivation, you'll find it easier to speak their language – and appeal to their criteria. So spot the motivations of those around you. If it's clear they're driven by a single motivator then your way forward is clear; if you sense they use a combination of motivators, you'll need to be a bit more flexible.

Getting together with an affiliator

To hit it off with an affiliator, give them all the gossip. They'll want to know what everyone else has been doing – so tell them. They'll want to talk about themselves and the other people they know – so ask them.

In particular, be upfront if you get on well with them – and never let them down socially. The worst thing you can do to an affiliator friend is to stand them up in favour of a work event. They'll take it to heart and think you don't care.

On the other hand, the affiliators you work with will try extra hard once they see you as a friend as well as a colleague. You can, in fact, build on this by making sure to have regular lunches or drinks with them, always remembering their birthdays and avoiding conflict like the plague.

Though be warned – if you do it cynically, for reasons of

achievement or influence, a true affiliator will spot that and mark you down. (An affiliator who also combines achievement or influence will know what you're doing, admire it and play right along.)

Affiliator anthem: You'll never walk alone (Gerry and The Pacemakers)

I've even known jobs won just by meeting an affiliator's criteria. One male friend of mine reported being interviewed for a job by a charming personnel officer who chatted to him for an hour about mutual interests until he was silently screaming at her to start discussing the work stuff; if she didn't have better things to do with her time, he certainly did.

But after exactly 55 minutes, this woman looked at her watch, announced she had a meeting on the hour and said 'You're hired!' She was an affiliator, so all that was important to her was whether he was her sort of person.

Big warning, though: you too may gel beautifully with that affiliator interviewee because they're often so socially competent – but can they do the job? Check before appointing. I remember once working with such a person. She spent most of the time on the phone and the only time she really got her head down was when she prepared a weekly 'get together' meal for everyone else in the office. Put it this way – as a book-keeper, she was a great hostess.

Doing your best for an achiever

To get on with someone who's largely an achiever, focus on success. So enquire what they've been doing in the last few months and when they tell you, home in on what they got right and celebrate with them. Also share your achievements with them – unless they're an influencer too, in which case they may feel threatened by your wins and won't want to know.

At work, an achiever boss will be seriously unhappy if you don't produce results. They'll agree with American steel tycoon James Ling 'Don't tell me how hard you work. Tell me how much you get done.'

This motto undoubtedly met with the full approval of the late Colin Chapman, founder of Britain's Lotus Cars. He was cool if his drivers came in last, because he knew that even a great deal of extra effort wouldn't make much difference to the result. But if a driver came in second or third, he'd never forgive them – because in his eyes, if they were that close to victory, they could have and should have won.

If you're managing an achiever, set clear goals and say clearly when those have been reached or missed. An achiever is usually happy to get feedback of whatever kind – so long as you make it clear just how your criticism is helping them to move on.

On the other hand, never give achievers a project where success is going to be uncertain as this demotivates them. So set clear goals, clock when they're reached and have a good loud celebration of that fact.

Making an impression on an influencer

You have two choices with people who are largely influencers – a clear yes and a clear no.

If the influencer is your boss or in any position of authority over you, then your best bet is usually to say 'yes'. Show them respect, don't argue, do things their way. And be sure you call them by whatever title they choose; they're an influencer, they'll have thought about that, even if their conclusion is to insist you call them by their first name!

Also remember that, though influencers can be unpopular, there are advantages to working with them. They're on top of office politics, they act as mine detectors on what's going down and they usually get what they want – bringing you the reflected glory.

Influence anthem: Under my thumb (The Rolling Stones)

But if an influencer is your peer – friend, colleague or partner – then in the interests of survival, you have to be prepared to say 'no', to take a firm stand, to insist on your rights. Don't try to get them to be nice to you, don't bother appealing to their better nature – a true influencer only really responds to an equal who acts like an equal. So neither back down nor start a fight. Because if you do, they'll lick their lips, pile in there and simply win.

Active influencers – those who want deliberate power over those around them – are not good news in a social context. They'll tend to spend the first part of the evening jockeying for position and the second part mixing it with anyone who challenges them.

But 'passive' influencers – those who watch power, rather than seeking it – will usually be up for endless gossip about who's high in the pecking order and who's sleeping with whom. Cultivate them – they're a lot of fun.

Motivation at work

When it comes to work, always make sure your personality patterns fit the job you do. Get that wrong and you'll be unfulfilled and miserable.

It's especially important to get it right with this particular personality pattern. Because, quite simply, if you choose a career direction that contradicts your McClelland motivator mode, you're going to be working against your deepest level of motivation

– and you're going to end up highly frustrated on a day-to-day level.

The bottom line is that you can't change a whole career structure – it's bigger than you are. So don't opt for one where there isn't at least a basic fit with your personality.

Affiliation-oriented careers

Affiliation jobs are people-centred. Think medicine, counselling, social work, teaching – the traditional 'caring services'. You don't necessarily need to be socially competent, although it helps if you are. What you do need is to be able to put people first – always. These careers can lead to burn-out because they are *soooo* draining of your time and compassion. But the rewards are many and colleagues are often caring and good to be around.

Achievement-oriented careers

Achievement jobs are results centred. Think manufacturing, accountancy, sales or any commission-based work where performance and product rule. The pace may be hard and fast, the emphasis on billable hours and results-related pay. Of course people matter, but they come second to the sales figures. These careers can be stressful because the hours and the effort needed are so demanding. But you do get an immense sense of self-esteem at having succeeded – and survived!

Influence-oriented careers

Influence jobs are about power over others. Think about the law, where the whole aim is to win over your opponent. Or politics, where cut and thrust is as usual as cooperation and respect. Or even advertising and the media, particularly hard news, where you are influencing the public – plus sometimes also trying to persuade interviewees to give you the story. The crunch here is that there can be a great deal of in-fighting and manipulation – you may need to be ruthless in order to survive.

Mix and match

Of course, few jobs are driven solely by one of these McClelland motivators. And subcategories of different careers can be powered by different mixtures. So a family lawyer will tend to add affiliation to the influence foundation – because of the more soft-centred nature of her work. A nursing administrator will need to add achievement to the affiliation foundation – or risk his hospital being bottom of the league table.

But in general, you do need to match basic bias with basic bias. Join an achievement-oriented profession when at heart you're an affiliator and you won't feel valued. Take up an affiliation career when at heart you're an achiever and you'll get frustrated at the lack of performance. Set off on an influence path if you're not a true influencer and you'll be excruciatingly uncomfortable because of all the conflict.

Plus, even if you are happy, your employers won't be. Be too achievement or influence-oriented in a heavily affiliation profession and you'll get the reputation of being hard. Be too affiliation-driven in achievement or influence careers – and you'll be marked down as soft.

Motivation at play

Motivation doesn't just kick in at work. It also affects you when you play.

So if someone's more affiliation-oriented, they'll do best at hobbies where people are valued. They may view competitive sports as cruel. And they'll be most motivated by the support of other people – going to a class, training with a friend, working with a personal coach.

If someone's more achievement-oriented, they'll want hobbies where they do well. Anything with a score will suit – either a competitive game or one where they compete against themselves to reach their highest potential. They'll set daily, weekly and even yearly goals and give themselves regular rewards for success.

If someone's more influence-oriented, they'll like hobbies where they make an impact. Or, at a pinch, where they can battle against the elements and take control that way. The real turn-on for them is being able to be in charge – so they may gravitate towards being a referee, a coach or, if all else fails, a committee member!

PS: Keeping the peace

 Never let two influencers muscle in on the same bit of a project. Whether planning a wedding or a sales drive, give them different areas to run.

Get one organizing the invites while the other sorts out the flowers. Get one managing the budget while the other manages the reps. If you don't, they'll spend all their time trying to muscle in on each other's patch – and you'll have to sort out the ensuing chaos.

what makes people tick?

Carrot or stick:
towards/away from strategy

(2) What gets us out of bed? What gets us up and doing day-to-day? Sure, affiliation, achievement and influence motivate us in a general sense, give our lives a sense of purpose. But underneath that, there's a much more specific motivation strategy.

And it's this. Are we driven more by goals or by problems? Are we compelled more by the carrots in life – or more by the sticks? Are we motivated 'towards' or 'away from'?

More towards motivation

Forty per cent of us are motivated more towards things than away from them. We'll bounce with excitement at the possibilities, the benefits, the rewards. We believe that 'somewhere over the rainbow' lie the goodies and we generate our energy from that.

And if we're seriously towards-motivated, we'll not even register any attached problems on the way. My friend Ben is a good example of this.

Want to know your own strategy? See page 254.

Several years ago, during the conflict in former Yugoslavia, he decided to drive to a small town in Croatia with a truck full of light bulbs – the issue being that communities there had electricity, but no means of utilizing it.

Ben spent three hard months getting sponsorship, fighting red tape and organizing the trip. Then he spent another sleepless week driving down to Croatia, delivering the bulbs and driving back.

When we met, a few days later, did Ben once mention the hardships? He did not. Instead he described the excitement of planning, the victory over bureaucracy, the people he met ... and how wonderful it was to drive out of that Croatian town and turn back to see it illuminated. His motivation – in fact, his entire view of life – was completely towards.

More away-from motivation

Forty per cent of us are motivated more away from things than towards them. What gets us going is fear of what we're going to lose. We work to avoid issues, ease difficulties, meet challenges. Frankly, we're problem-driven. We don't necessarily expect the worst – but we do get the buzz from finding solutions.

The most away-from-motivated person I ever knew was a superb holiday tour guide. She was good precisely because she foresaw all the problems her group could meet – for her, prevention was better than cure and she was the one who was going to do the preventing.

So if problems arose – as they always did, of course – she was driven to fix them. She was a swan – calm and cool on the surface – where her tourist clients could see her, but paddling away like fury beneath to ensure the hotels were perfect, the food amazing and every flight left on time.

When, where, how?

No one's motivated completely towards or completely away-from; we all combine the two. We all drive ourselves with a combination of wanting to succeed, be rich, be happy and wanting not to fail, be poor, be miserable.

Here are some classic combinations that you might find:

- You can be towards-motivated in one context, away-from-motivated in another. I've a colleague who's towards-motivated at work – driven by the desire to see a good job well done. But she's away-from-motivated at home – ignoring the cleaning until the chaos of her house finally pushes her over the edge.
- You can have both motivations in a single context. On a regular visit to the dentist, you're driven both by the towards motivation of wanting healthy teeth and the away-from of avoiding tooth decay.
- You may be driven by towards motivation in one emotional state, away-from motivation in another. A quick straw poll among my friends revealed that we do things in towards-motivated mode when feeling good, in away-from mode when stressed. When on top, we buy clothes for sheer joy. When we're feeling low, we shop to ease the emotional pain.
- Faced with something new or strange, you may briefly switch to 'away-from'. Because given a new car to drive or new baby to care for, problem-awareness is sensible – it wouldn't do to get it

wrong. When you've mastered what you're doing – changing gear or changing nappies – you'll switch back into your normal, more balanced, strategy.

- Over something you have a strong investment in, you may switch to 'away from' – because you get very scared of getting it wrong. Once you know things are going to work out, you switch back to your normal strategy.

- You may switch motivations over time. At eighteen, a friend and I loved chatting up boys – every night was totally motivated towards enjoyment. But I met her recently and her motivation has changed. Two divorces on, her dating has a sadder edge to it – she's now running away from being alone.

A perfect motivation strategy?

When it comes to motivation, which is better? Towards? Or away from? They both have their pros and cons.

If you're more towards

The joy of mainly towards motivation strategies is that they keep you positive while you're aiming for something. Budding actors have to be largely towards-motivated – towards the glowing vision of being famous – because there's such a small chance of success, they need serious positivity to keep them going.

But the problem with extremely towards-motivated people is that they tend to take absolutely no account of the downside. So you may simply not be aware of problems – just not take them into account.

Plus, a completely towards motivation can mean you never stop and enjoy anything. Sure you get motivated by a towards goal – like the job or the lover you just know will be perfect for you. But when you've got the job or seduced the lover, the original towards motivation isn't in operation any more. Result? An instant need to move on, towards the next goal.

If you're more away from

Mainly away-from motivation strategies are great to get you problem-solving. If you're buying a second-hand car or a new house, then away-from will be useful in ways that towards motivation never can be, letting you spot the problems rather than get over-enthusiastic and rush into an unwise purchase.

But you can end up distracted into firefighting – all the time. In work, this may mean you're always troubleshooting, never developing. In love, it may mean you compulsively try to make your relationship better and end up having 'we need to talk' interactions with your partner every night.

There's also a nasty little twist on away-from, which will make your life hell. You get motivated by an away-from goal – like working hard solely on the motivation of avoiding poverty. But once you get some money and the fear of the breadline fades, the away-from motivation dims. And then you're left just cruising; without motivation – and without any get up and go.

The perfect motivation strategy

To be honest, towards-motivated people are, in general, happier bunnies than away-from-motivated people, because they concentrate on the things that make them feel excited and enthusiastic rather than the things that make them feel wary and anxious.

But to motivate yourself perfectly, you do need both the carrot and the stick. Because one of the secrets of highly motivated people is that they don't rely only on the glow of the goodies or only on the fear of failure to keep them going. They mix the two.

The perfect motivation strategy goes like this.

- Set your towards motivation goal – what you really want. By thinking about it, talking about it, dreaming about it, get to a point where it's really compelling.
- Boost your towards motivation by reminding yourself of how you've succeeded in the past, in this or other linked areas.
- Become aware of your away-from reasons – what you're trying to avoid. Don't dwell on these things, but do let them spur you on.
- Use your away-from motivation to spot potential problems in reaching your goal. Troubleshoot these early so the path to your goal is clear.
- Then take the first step.

Getting a balance

If you've got a balance of towards and away-from motivation, you'll find the above-mentioned strategy easy. So if you want to lose weight, you'll use your towards motivation to get a compelling picture of the new slim you and you'll use your away-from motivation to avoid tempting food.

But if you're strongly towards- or strongly away-from-motivated, you may find it hard to run that perfect motivation strategy.

Here's how to succeed.

To get a balanced strategy if you're biased towards:
- Practise thinking about problems you may meet on the way to your goal. List at least three difficulties – then resist your usual temptation to discount them. Instead, treat them as a chance to get a better, more compelling result.
- Get some coaching from an away-from motivated person – ask them how they spot problems ahead of time, how they plan

their escape routes, how they do downside planning without getting demotivated.

- When you reach a goal, be aware that to keep it rewarding and compelling, you need to keep putting energy in; don't lose interest when you reach your aim.

To get a balanced strategy if you're biased away-from:
- Practise thinking about your goal in positives. List at least three compelling aspects of what you're aiming for – then resist your usual temptation to start thinking of the downside. Instead, use the optimism to help you perform better.
- Get some coaching from a towards-motivated person – ask them how they set positive goals as well as negative ones. Pick up on their enthusiasm and use it as an energy source.
- When you reach a goal, allow yourself to enjoy and appreciate it. You've done the work. You deserve a pat on the back. Relax. Enjoy.

Bridging the motivation gap

Get strongly towards-motivated people and away-from motivated people in the same room – let alone the same project or the same marriage – and they're likely to affect each other – badly. The reason for this is that if you're a towards-motivated person, then listening to an away-from talk can make you feel really low – they always seem to be noticing negatives and problems.

On the other hand, if you're away-from, then a towards-motivated person will make you feel insecure – they come across as total Polyannas who never take into account what might go wrong, so are probably heading for disaster.

In order to bridge the gap, try to understand what your opposite number feels – what their hopes and fears are, what drives them on.

Towards-motivated person: 'I imagine how good I'll feel when I've finished the kitchen units ... my partner's face when we've finally got things looking good.'

For example, to really inspire a towards-motivated person – whether partner or employee – you need to tap into their fascination with the rewards, the positives. You need to get them enthused about what's going to happen, create a vision of a bright future.

But you'll also need to watch their backs. As the old saying runs 'your lack of foresight does not constitute my emergency' – but in fact, if you're dealing with a towards-motivated person, it may well constitute your emergency, because chances are they won't have had any foresight at all. So be careful with the client who, in the first meeting, is over the moon with what you have in mind, but never mentions any downside. He's probably highly towards-motivated – and it'll be up to you to build in fall-back plans.

Away-from-motivated person: 'I imagine not finishing the kitchen units ... my partner's face getting darker. It's a gut-wrenching feeling I'll do anything to avoid.'

Conversely, to really motivate an away-from, you need to point out that following a particular course of action will make their life easier, will avoid specific future problems.

Plus, you need to be aware that they'll find it difficult to be positive; they're constantly on the look-out for traps and minefields – and that may make them sound picky and critical. In particular – very soul-destroying this – they may only be able to tell you what they don't want in your work.

The experience of a young programmer of my acquaintance illustrates the point perfectly. He prepared a piece of work for a very prestigious client who was also extremely away-from. My young colleague had a first stab at the work – and the client then

what makes people tick?

realized that she didn't want what he'd done. So he did it again. And again. Every time she took what he had done and moved 'away from' it, until at last, in despair, he threw in the towel. He says he has no idea whether they ever got anybody to complete the job. He does know that he personally should have given up after the third try.

And the conclusion? People who work very closely together – in business or in love – typically end up developing complementary motivation strategies. Even if they both start off with mixed strategies, they'll polarize so that one ends up more towards-motivated and the other more away-from.

The best example of this I ever saw was during supper with a good friend of mine and her husband. She has always struck me as a very towards-motivated person, almost too much so; she gets starry-eyed about every possibility. Then I met him – and I realized why.

For every towards-motivated comment she made, he would add an away-from. When she said how delicious the fish looked, he suggested we checked if it was fresh. When she offered to buy some wine, he rushed in to offer to abstain and drive us all home.

It wasn't that he was pessimistic – he shared her optimism about the good fish and the fine wine. But he spent all his time covering our backs, making sure that nothing went wrong. I began to see why my friend can be so towards-motivated. She isn't motivated by fear of anything because her husband has that one fully covered.

The moral of this tale? If you and your partner (or friend, or colleague) have different approaches when it comes to motivation, don't resist. Go with it. Because the perfect motivation strategy is balanced, towards and away-from – and if each of you provides one element, together you have the set.

Carrot jobs, stick jobs

$ Most people combine towards and away-from. And actually, so do most jobs. To hold down any kind of post you need to be both motivated by the goodies and willing to solve the problems.

That said, some jobs are strongly towards-motivated. They rely on you having a compelling vision, they need you to get a goal and be enthused by it, to keep going regardless.

Good jobs for towards-motivated people: sales rep, entrepreneur, inventor, designer.

Other jobs are strongly biased away-from. They need you to be aware of what can go wrong, to monitor, cost-cut, do risk assessment or otherwise solve problems. Book-keeping is a classic away-from job – you'll fall on your face at a rate of knots if as a book-keeper you happily admire the totals that are correct and don't spot the ones that aren't!

The fact that any job is ever away-from-motivated may surprise you. Because most people naturally assume that everyone is motivated by the positive – rewards, bonuses, targets. Wrong. If you're away-from, you'll actually find more fulfilment in spotting and solving the negative – in feeling that you've avoided problems, side-stepped crises.

Good jobs for away-from people: editor, health and safety administrator, complaints handler.

I recently watched a TV interview with James Dyson, inventor of the British Dyson home-cleaning equipment. Now, I've always imagined that inventors were aglow with an exciting vision of what they could achieve. But listening to Dyson talk, all I heard were

what makes people tick?

things like 'Well, I realized that normal vacuum cleaners don't really suck the dust up – so I sorted that' ... 'I looked at normal washing machines and there wasn't a lot going on – so I wanted to solve that problem.' I realized that James is away-from, utterly.

Mixing motivations can lead to trouble when it comes to team working. If you land a job where you're strongly motivated one way and the rest of the group are strongly motivated the other way, watch out for conflict. Yes, you're invaluable, because you provide the balance – every career arena needs a little of both motivational strategies. But because you're the odd one out, others may ignore you. Don't take the mismatch personally. Do put energy into influencing the result. Do believe you have something to offer.

A final interesting point: it's not just jobs that are towards- or away-from-motivated, but employers too. Towards-motivated employers give you things to aim for – bonuses, commission, promotion or a series of little emerald chips on a gold brooch to wear on your uniform. Away-from employers give you things to avoid – the threat of falling sales figures or temper tantrums from the boss. If your company is kept on red alert by constant threat of redundancy then you work for an away-from-motivated firm. (And the moral of this tale is that if you want to be happy working for a company, you'll go for a fit between their motivational approach and yours.)

What are you motivated towards?

You can be driven towards absolutely anything in life. But there are some classics – things about which lots of people are towards-motivated.

So when you're interacting with people, when you turn on the television, when you skim a magazine, when you tackle a task ... you could be pulled towards any number of things – you notice them, pay attention to them, feel good about them.

- **Knowledge-towards:** You agree with Benjamin Disraeli when he said, 'The most successful man in life is the man who has the best information.' You may back that up by collecting dates, times, names, details, numbers – you're probably the 'list junkie' on your block.
- **Object-towards:** You love things for their own sake. It isn't that you necessarily value objects above people or are materialistic or mercenary. But you love items for their beauty, their history, their craftsmanship, their value.
- **Ideas-towards:** You love debating the principles of things, talking about the theory behind some new invention. You echo Victor Hugo when he said, 'There's one thing stronger than all the armies in the world and that is an idea whose time has come.'
- **Systems-towards:** You're fascinated by what makes the world go round. You explore processes, interrelationships, links. You might love analysing your relationship ... or taking apart an alarm clock.
- **Feelings-towards:** You notice the emotion in things. It isn't always that you yourself want to feel strongly; it might be that you notice when other people do – or when a book, play or poem deals with emotion.
- **Utility-towards:** You'll notice first what's useful. If you can't find a direct function for any information, person or thing, you lose interest. You're not exploitative – it's just that if something's not useful, your mind wanders.
- **Action-towards:** You'll sympathize with Alexander the Great who, when fighting his way round the Turkish coast in 333BC, found a huge headland in his way and simply walked his army into the sea and round the offending hill. Sure, he drowned a good proportion of his men, but at least they kept moving. Your attention is drawn to doing and you tend to keep busy, busy, busy.

Here's an example of different people's towards motivations. I remember as a teenager, sitting on the rocks at sunset, watching a fabulous sea view in the company of a boyfriend. I – an emotions-towards – was feeling warm and gooey. What I didn't know was that he – a systems-towards – was busy doing something completely different with his mind.

'What are you thinking?' I asked. He hesitated just long enough for me to imagine that I was going to get a romantic reply. Then he said, 'I was just wondering how the tidal current round here operates.'

The dull clunk to be heard at that moment was the sound of two incompatible strategies totally failing to engage.

What that story shows is that like my teenage beau and I, you and the people around you are likely to have different towards motivations, in different priority order. That lad wasn't completely uninterested in emotion; it just wasn't top of his priority list at the time I asked my question. Whereas for me – particularly in that context – it was.

You'll know immediately you hit a clash of towards motivations. You'll wonder what on earth the other person is on about; you'll experience a slow flush of confusion or irritation. The answer is to get curious, not defensive. Yes, someone else has different values from you. So what? Be interested. Listen. Ask questions. Learn.

Or, if you really want to get something from the experience, ask the other person to give you the benefit of the specialism that their towards motivation gives them. And make use of that. So, wherever you can ...

- **brain-hoover a knowledge-towards friend for the latest info on anything**
- **take an object-towards person shopping with you because they know where to go and what to buy**

- **call an ideas or systems-towards person at the start of a project, when you need to brainstorm how things are going to work**
- **ring a feelings-towards person for support when you're feeling ecstatic or desperate**
- **get a utility or action-towards person when you want things done – ask them to move house for you and watch the tea chests empty as if by magic!**

And now, a commercial break

$ Surely advertisements are always towards motivated? They hook people who want the sizzle in the sausage and are prepared to pay for it. Right?

Not always. Some products naturally appeal to away-from-motivated personalities. Insurance, private health, loan agencies – adverts for these are aimed at those who register looming disaster. These ads sell by reminding us how life can go wrong, then providing the solution – their service.

Plus, many seemingly towards-motivated ads slide in a bit of away-from so that they can target the widest variety of people. So car ads major on the style, speed and sex appeal (towards) but also the way a motor avoids breakdowns, accidents and high fuel consumption (away-from).

The following is a classic example of successful away-from marketing. Computer giant Microsoft realized that many corporate purchasers were scared of making buying decisions on hardware in case they got it wrong and were fired. So they instituted a marketing plan known as FUD – fear, uncertainty and doubt. Every ad subtly suggested that buying Microsoft was by far the safest decision – with heavy hints that buying any other brand would undoubtedly result in one blowing out one's entire career.

what makes people tick?

The away-from-motivated buyers got the message and flocked in droves to buy the product.

PS: Instant diagnosis 1

Want a quick way of spotting someone's towards/away-from pattern?

When someone explains why they're doing something, what they say after the word 'because' will tell you. If the words after 'because' are positive goals, then they're towards-motivated. If the words after 'because' are negative problems, then they're away-from-motivated. For example – they're on a diet: is that *because* they want to look gorgeous (towards) or *because* they don't want to look fat (away-from)?

Hence, to discover motivation, simply ask someone a question about 'why' they did something. Then listen to what emerges after the word 'because'.

HOW PERSONALITY WORKS 1

Is your personality set before you pop out of the womb? Or after? Answer – both. Because, yes, some personality patterns are inherited. Twins usually grow up with some basic character similarities even if they've been brought up separately. And adopted siblings will often grow up with different patterns even if they've been brought up together.

But genetics isn't the whole story. There are still huge amounts of personality that are learned: learned by modelling parents and siblings; learned from friends, lovers, colleagues; learned by being rewarded for some things and punished for others.

And then, as you get older, heredity and environment combine with a human tendency to opt for the comfortable. And the result is you gravitate towards situations which feel natural, which play to your personality strengths and sidestep your weaknesses. And doing that reinforces your personality all over again.

For example, you're born an introvert so you don't mix much at nursery school. As a result, you don't get to practise being at ease with other children. So you don't get to feel massively comfortable around people. So you grow up avoiding groups, meetings, parties. So you stay introverted.

Personality isn't just what you're born with. It's also what you learn.

Being who you are: self-esteem scale

3 Right down at the bottom, on the bedrock of our personality, is one fundamental pattern, the pattern that tells us how much we're worth: self-esteem.

If we've got self-esteem, it doesn't mean to say we're full of ourselves. What we are is at ease with ourselves. We know our strengths and we're comfortable with our weaknesses. We feel good about our own identity, we have a positive concept of ourselves.

Be clear here. We're not only talking about feeling good because we've had a success or a win. Self-esteem is about who we are – not about what we do. So people with low self-esteem can do a superb job but still not feel valid. Those with high self-esteem – who typically perform well because they're at ease with themselves – will nevertheless still do badly from time to time. But they never take it to heart. They never believe that they're a failure as a person just because they've had a failure in life.

Want to know where you fall on this scale? See page 256.

So even if everything goes wrong, high self-esteem people bounce back, keep going, keep believing that they're OK. That doesn't mean they're self-obsessed. On the contrary, they've a lot of attention to spare for other people – because they're not frenetically keeping themselves on an even keel.

One of the 'highest self-esteem' men I know spent the whole of our first meeting finding out about everyone else round the table – with genuine fascination. I learned later that he's a top charity worker, who's raised literally millions of pounds for good causes and set up dozens of support schemes for people in need. In other words, this guy has every reason in the world to spend the whole evening talking about himself. But he didn't. He's sufficiently sure of his own value to have tons of attention left over for other people. He already knows he's worth it.

And then there's the other side of the coin. People with low self-esteem don't know they're worth it. And that bubbling feeling of failure creates a whole Pandora's box of vulnerabilities. They choose goals that are too low and so underachieve. They set goals that are too high and then give up. They spend their time hesitating, apologizing, defending – pumping up their achievements to get attention, excusing their failures to get reassurance. Or killing the pain with drink, food, drugs and whatever else will get them through the night.

Low self-esteem people don't do all this for the fun of it. They do it because they don't like themselves and they need to compensate by getting other people to do the liking for them. So they'll concentrate on themselves to the exclusion of others and – unlike my charity friend – they'll spend three solid hours telling you about themselves without drawing breath. Aaarggh!

A final point on self-esteem. Quite simply, it makes or breaks all the other personality patterns. If we have low self-esteem, then however superb our character is otherwise, we won't fulfil our potential. Our talents won't come to the fore because we'll feel bad about them, hide them or undermine them.

But if we have high self-esteem, then all the other aspects of our personality will shine.

You're like this because ...

 A newborn doesn't have high esteem or low esteem. Newborns just are.

But what happens then is crucial. Because it's what happens after the umbilical cord is cut that dictates how the baby feels about itself. It's what happens as the child grows up that dictates whether the adult believes he or she is OK. Sure, events in adult life will boost or undermine esteem – but they can only build on whatever foundation has been laid in childhood.

So if someone has low self-esteem, it's often because when they were a child, parents, teachers, relatives and friends ...

- **had so many expectations that the child constantly felt s/he was failing**
- **had so few expectations that the child felt no one believed in him/her**
- **gave the message that the child was useless or unwanted**
- **felt bad about themselves so that the child modelled low self-esteem**
- **made the child feel they were the odd one out**
- **were unhappy themselves and made the child think s/he was to blame for that**
- **ill-treated the child, who then thought s/he deserved ill treatment**
- **felt helpless themselves, teaching the child that s/he couldn't overcome setbacks**

On the other hand, if someone has high self-esteem, it's often because when they were a child, parents, teachers, relatives and friends ...

- **had balanced expectations, so the child was challenged but succeeded**
- **told the child what s/he was good at**
- **showed the child that s/he was loved**
- **felt good about themselves so that the child modelled high self-esteem**
- **made the child feel included**
- **even when they were unhappy, made it clear that wasn't the child's fault**

- **treated the child well, so s/he thought s/he deserved good treatment**
- **showed the child that setbacks can be overcome**

Boosting others' feelgood factor

Is there someone in your life with low self-esteem? Someone who just doesn't believe they're worthwhile? Someone who runs a battery of timid or nervous or overcompensating behaviours? There is a way to help them.

First, though, an explanation. American psychologists did two studies with children. In the first study, the aim was to get the children to be tidier. In the second study, the aim was to get the children to improve their maths.

In both studies, half the children were rewarded with praise when they put in a good performance – were tidy or improved their maths scores. And half the children were simply told, three or four times, that they were tidy children or that they were the kind of children who worked hard at maths.

Spot the difference? In the first group, children were receiving a reward for the specific act of getting it right. In the second group, they were being told that they were the sort of person who naturally got it right.

Guess which groups did best? Sure, the first group improved. But the second group scored an average of 10 per cent higher right across the board.

Why? Well, if you reward someone for their success – be that working hard or scoring goals – then they'll learn to work hard and score goals. But they'll also learn that when they don't work or score goals, the reward simply stops. In the end, you have to keep rewarding or they'll stop performing. And sometimes, you even have to up the reward in order to keep them performing.

But if you give someone a good feeling about their identity – tell

what makes people tick?

Low self-esteem.   High self-esteem.

them that they're a hard-working person, a good goal-scorer – then it really beds in. They start thinking of themselves as that sort of person. They start to generalize and believe it. And then, miraculously, they start to act like that sort of person in every context and through all sorts of behaviours.

They don't need rewarding every time. They don't need praise every single occasion. They just spontaneously start to believe in their own positive identity. They start to generate their own, internal feelgood factor.

So if you want your partner, relative, friend or child to have high self-esteem, don't simply reward them when they do well. Instead, tell them – genuinely – when you are aware of them being the sort of person who is wonderful, clever, beautiful, brave, loving ...

If you believe in someone's positive identity and you tell them that, then they will start to believe in their positive identity too. And then their self-esteem will blossom.

Boosting your personal feelgood factor

However high your self-esteem, at some point it'll take a tumble. A rotten job choice, a bad love affair or just a horrid day at work ... may all make you lick your wounds. So don't be surprised if your self-esteem varies wildly under certain circumstances.

When that happens, you'll need some instant boosters. Here are seven of the boosters that – over a long career in the personal development field – I've found work best.

Seven short-term self-esteem boosters
- Treat yourself to something you want – a walk in the park, a favourite video, a luxurious bath, a good book. Do this 100 per cent, to the max and without guilt and you will feel better.
- Get a professional makeover – or do-it-yourself by sorting your wardrobe and revamping your style. Feeling good about the way you look outside will improve the way you feel inside. (It will never sort a deep lack of self-esteem though, which is why even supermodels do drugs.)
- Shift your body language. A recent study at the University of Madison suggests that just a simple grin will nudge your brain into boosting your 'feelgood' factor. So act as if you like yourself – stand tall, move confidently, keep eye contact and smile, smile, smile.
- If you know you can handle the responsibility, buy a pet. They'll respond to you for who you are, no holding back. Plus, the fact that you're caring for them – and that they're grateful for your care – will prove to you that you are worthwhile.
- Get some touch – a hug, a massage, a pedicure or manicure. Touch lowers blood pressure, boosts the immune system, makes you feel good in and about yourself. (The exception is sex without

affection, which often leaves you feeling even worse than before.)

- Get a trusted friend, relative or lover to compliment you genuinely. Write down what they say – and keep that record so you can return to it when the bad times hit again.
- Take charge. Make a decision you've been putting off. Take some action you've been hesitating over. Be honest with someone around whom you've previously held back. If you get back in control of what's happening, you'll get back in control of your self-esteem.

Sometimes, low self-esteem is a bit more than a temporary thing. It's lasted a while – or you know that it's a deep-rooted part of your personality. Here are three of the solutions I've found work best with more heavy-duty self-doubt.

Three heavy-duty self-esteem raisers
- Spot where you're giving yourself negative messages 'I'm fat. I'm stupid. I'm unlovable.' ... List them, then opposite each write a contradiction – 'I'm the right weight. I'm bright. I deserve love.' – to 'reprogramme' your brain with new beliefs. The book *Mind over Mood* (page 293) is an excellent guide to this effective form of self-help.
- If the key brain chemical serotonin is low, your confidence will plummet. Ways of increasing serotonin include: avoiding stress; taking vitamin B, magnesium and selenium supplements; indulging in regular exercise; getting enough sunlight, particularly in winter. Plus, have yourself checked for allergies, and don't hesitate to visit your GP if you feel low for more than 14 days.
- If the above doesn't shift stuff, or if you know that you've had life experiences that have left you vulnerable, then see a counsellor and sort it, right now. (For further details, sees the Resources section on page 293.)

PS: Group self-esteem

 A good way of raising the self-esteem of a group is to give them a challenge.

It needs to be a challenge that is non-trivial – so not just sorting paper clips, but getting them to work on a revolutionary new design for a paper clip. And it needs to be a challenge they can overcome but with difficulty – so not just going out for a country stroll, but supporting each other through an outward bound course.

A group that wins out in that situation will learn, at a very deep level, that they can succeed. And mysteriously this will raise their self-esteem – and so shift their entire personalities.

Sunshine or showers:
optimism/pessimism strategy

(4) Do we see the glass as half full? Or half empty? Do we tend to see the best in life? Or the worst? In other words, is our personality based on emotional optimism or pessimism?

More optimistic

If all our clouds have silver linings, then we're optimistic. We look back at the past and think it was for the best. We look forward to the future and expect that things will turn out fine. We look at what's happening and put a positive spin on it, regardless.

It was optimist John F. Kennedy who, commenting on a scary 7 per cent unemployment figure, pointed out that it meant 93 per cent of people were still working. An optimist keeps hoping – and, yes, sometimes does that against all odds. Because optimism can lead to sheer folly. An optimist is the one who, with no previous track record, goes to Hollywood for the winter, every winter, to work the tables and 'get spotted'. An optimist, is the one who, despite knowing their new lover's previous track record, convinces themselves that he'll be faithful this time. Naive? Yes, often.

Want to know your own strategy? See page 259.

He who limps ... is still walking. (Polish poet and optimist Stanislaw J. Lec)

On the other hand, optimists are great at work because the fact they think things are going to go well puts a smile on their face and in their voice. And they're more likely to make a basically sound

Optimist. Pessimist.

relationship work simply because they don't get all neurotic worrying that it won't.

That said, an off-the-scale optimist can drive their spouse crazy because they think it'll take a single weekend to move house when packing the contents of the bathroom has already taken five days. I know. I was that spouse.

More pessimistic

If we tend to think it'll rain on the parade, then we're more pessimistic. We'll filter out what's positive, filter in what's negative. We'll see opportunities as problems. We'll look gift-horses in the mouth.

Pessimism isn't just about looking ahead in order to avoid things going wrong; it's about looking around and expecting things to go wrong. And it isn't confined to our own actions – we can be pessimistic on behalf of others, or about life, the universe and everything.

So we'll worry when we take out a loan – in case we can't repay

what makes people tick?

it. We'll worry when our partner gets a promotion – in case they can't hack it. We'll worry that our cough is terminal lung cancer (unsurprisingly, pessimists are often hypochondriacs too).

The optimist believes that we live in the best of all possible worlds. The pessimist fears this is true. (American songwriter Irving Caesar)

We may, in fact, never be happy unless we're worrying – because at least then we know we're on the case. The only time we relax is when something bad does happen, because then we've been proved right.

All of which makes pessimism sound the pits. And it can be an unhappy personality pattern to have. Recent studies have shown that it's much more realistic to be pessimistic; pessimists have a more accurate view of what's happening in the world. But in terms of what feels good, then optimism wins out all the time, every time.

You're like this because ...

Are optimists and pessimists born or made? There's certainly evidence that as early as six months old, babies respond enthusiastically or warily. The little pessimists are suspicious of the world, the tiny optimists hopeful about it. And that's before they can even talk.

But childhood experience also has a lot to answer for. If parents are hopeful, the child is too. If parents label their offspring as 'glum' or 'always got a face on her', the child picks up that identity and runs with it.

Plus, unsurprisingly, if childhood is full of insults or abuse, then pessimism is more likely in later life; if full of support and cuddles then the resulting adult is more likely to be an optimist.

But those expectations may well be shifted, particularly in the negative direction, by later life events. So whatever age you are, an accident, a bereavement, a rejection or a loss can pull the rug from under your hopeful world view.

Of course, it can work the other way. If something wonderful happens, you can suddenly put on the rose-coloured glasses rather than taking them off. Falling in reciprocal love is the classic. The thought that this wonderful person also thinks you're wonderful can be enough to reverse even the most entrenched pessimism – if only for a while.

The optimist sees opportunity in every danger. The pessimist sees danger in every opportunity. (WWII Prime Minister Winston Churchill)

Why optimism is best

Optimism doesn't just feel better. It also works better.

- A study begun in 1953 tracked a group of college students for 35 years. For 20 years after college, there was no difference in their health. After that, the pessimists were more likely to be ill.
- A 1980 study followed 122 men who had their first heart attack. Eight years later, 21 of the 25 most pessimistic ones were no longer alive. Only six of the most optimistic ones had died.
- A 1984 study of 500 students showed that their optimism was more important than their academic grades in predicting success. Quite simply, the optimistic students did better.
- A 1990 study suggests that in the insurance business, pessimists quit at twice the rate of optimists. And optimists do 57 per cent better than pessimists by the time they've been in the job two years.

what makes people tick?

Learning to be helpless

There's a nasty personality variation on pessimism. It's called 'learned helplessness' and it goes like this.

You take a basic pessimistic personality, highly aware of painful possibilities. Then you add a subtle mix of mental conditions such as depression – and all of a sudden the person flips over into feeling there's nothing they can do to challenge disaster, so they give up.

It's a syndrome often found in prisoners of war or kidnap victims, who are literally powerless. But on a slightly less dramatic level, if you've ever met a classic 'drop out', who can't seem to find a job or a partner and spends their time watching endless TV re-runs, then that's what's happened to them – they've learned to be helpless. It can lead to rock-bottom self-esteem, not to mention a whole nasty little list of physical ailments and immune system disorders.

This is the way learned helplessness works ...

- **a person sees the worst in something**
- **s/he personalizes, takes all the responsibility**
- **then globalizes, feels bad not just for what s/he's done, but for who s/he is**
- **then generalizes, feels that nothing is right**
- **then future-generalizes, believes nothing will ever be right**
- **then gives in, stops trying to change things, concentrates on surviving**
- **and sometimes, believes it's not even worthwhile surviving**

If you're living or working with someone who seems to be tipping into this kind of abyss, then get help for them urgently. One good route is cognitive behavioural therapy, which has a number of techniques to challenge negative thoughts; see the Resources section on page 293.

But also, to stop yourself tumbling into this horrendous spiral, it's a good idea to actively develop these more positive approaches to life ...

- **when you get something right, tell yourself that it's all down to you**
- **when you get it right again, keep telling yourself how well you did**
- **when things go wrong, see it as a specific, reversible setback**
- **if things go wrong again, put that down to circumstances, not to you as a person**
- **if things carry on going wrong, keep believing they can change**
- **always act to solve problems: don't accept anything less than a good life**

If you're a dyed-in-the-wool pessimist – or tipping over into serious learned helplessness – then it may feel very scary to start putting in place techniques like these which will, by definition, make things seem brighter. It may quite simply feel wrong – because in your view, pessimism is the natural order of things.

But hang in there. Just give it a go. After all, if it doesn't work for you, you can always revert to how you were before.

PS: Mixing it

In any group including optimists and pessimists – and that means almost any group – prepare for the following scenario.

The optimists generate a glowing vision – which promptly panics the pessimists. The pessimists murmur doom and gloom – which promptly frustrates the optimists.

If you spot this happening in a group you're working with, then take action – or the whole thing will spiral out of control and into serious bad feeling. To keep the peace, make certain you reassure the pessimists with good downside planning and keep the optimists' enthusiasm high with talk of bright and glorious futures.

How high can you go?
Sensation-seeking scale

(5) University of Delaware, 1969, and Professor Martin Zuckerman is busy discovering a neat new personality pattern. He defines it as the human need for 'novel, varied, complex and intense' experiences. He calls it 'sensation seeking'.

In other words, this personality pattern describes how emotionally positive we feel about sensation – or how much it turns us off.

Want to know where you fall on this scale? See page 261.

If we're lower on the pattern, we're actually quite happy not to have adventures – we like things simple and safe. If we're higher on the pattern, we'll tend to walk on the wild side – and get bored to distraction if asked to live a normal life.

Sensation-seeking actually comes in four flavours.

- *Risk seeking:* a tendency to love physical challenge, such as snowboarding, rap-running and freefall base-jumping off Angel Falls.
- *Novelty seeking*: a liking for travel, meeting unusual people, living an unconventional lifestyle.
- *Boredom avoidance:* hating routine in anything and needing a job in particular to be a challenge.
- *Rule breaking*: a tendency to drift towards anything forbidden that society has to offer.

If we're high in one of these kinds of sensation-seeking, we're likely to be high in another. But not always – witness the white-water rafter who's never tasted alcohol or the heavy drug user who regards crossing the road as risky.

How does sensation-seeking affect us? At work, the lower we are

 what makes people tick?

in this pattern, the more likely we are to go for jobs that are quiet, routine, straightforward, undemanding. The higher we are, the more likely we'll be to sign up as a test pilot because we like risk or as a journalist because we like novelty. And if that doesn't stretch us, we'll unconsciously push ourselves too far and too fast, working long hours, loving the adrenalin burst that a really vicious deadline provides.

When it comes to interpersonals, the more we seek sensation in the novelty strand, the more likely we are to go for unconventional relationships – and if we're particularly high on rule breaking, we'll accompany those with large doses of illegal substances.

When it comes to love, our sensation-seeking score determines just how much we're drawn to emotional intensity, emotional involvement – or just sheer emotional risk.

And when it comes to sex, sensation-seeking affects whether we're likely to have a rich fantasy life, want sexual variation, stack up the numbers – and take gambles. One of my high-sensation-seeking male friends regularly invites a lady home with him at precisely the times when his committed partner is expected back – because the high he gets from wondering whether he's going to be discovered is (and I quote) 'like having adrenalin injected directly into my nervous system ...'

But sensation-seeking isn't necessarily a sign of being 'mad, bad or dangerous to know', because everyone seeks sensation of one sort or another. It's just a question of how much, how far and how fast.

A sensation-seeker tends to love people-stimulation like an extrovert does (page 144).

You're like this because ...

How do you get to be sensation-seeking? Recent research suggests it could be physiologically-based. A variety of American and Israeli studies from 1964 to the present day suggest that there are links with ...

- **genetic make-up – meaning that if you're a sensation-seeker, you are genetically programmed to need novelty in order to feel good**
- **unusually low levels of pleasure regulator monoamine oxidase B – meaning that you need more arousing activities to get the same pleasure as other people do**

But being a sensation-seeker may owe as much to our life as to our genes. So growing up in a sensation-seeking household may mean we follow suit, but growing up in a repressed household may mean we turn sensation-seeker just to spite. And if at school we fall in with sensation-seekers, we'll probably run with the crowd. Meanwhile, when we have kids and suddenly need to consider someone else's life as well as our own, we'll probably slow down.

One final point: the original research on sensation-seeking suggested that males were more likely to have a higher score than females. Some experts have suggested that this is genetic – that

what makes people tick?

men are programmed to be more sensation-seeking than women. But hold on a minute. Look around. Think of women soldiers in the front line, women executives in stressful jobs. Think of Ellen McArthur sailing round the world. (And rising levels of female smoking, drinking, drug abuse and sexual experimentation.)

A sensation-seeker tends to live here and now like a present-oriented person does (page 62).

So why the change? Maybe female physiology is shifting. More likely, women's genetic need for sensation has always been high – but it's only now we've got the freedom, the independence and the resources to indulge it.

The bottom line is that women still lag behind men in this personality pattern. But, for better or worse, we're catching up fast.

A fate worse than death?

See the term 'high-sensation-seeker', and the phrase 'drugs, sex and rock and roll' inexorably comes to mind. So are all sensation-seekers driving themselves into an early grave or an early prison sentence?

Not at all. If their need is just for complexity of input – sensation-seekers often like heavy rock music and horror films – then they're not exactly going to be putting their lives in danger. And if their need is just for physical stimulation then they may actually test atypically low on neuroticism, depression and anxiety and exceptionally high on emotional stability.

Specifically, if their need is for physical risk, a high-sensation-seeker may actually be safe in dangerous situations because pushing the boundaries engages them completely. So, whilst the low-sensation-seeker is panicking and making terminal mistakes, the high-sensation-seeker is on task and coping. One of the most emotionally phlegmatic guys I know drives at 100mph, snowboards off-piste 'steep 'n' deep' and is planning to sail round the world. Never had an accident. Never broken a bone.

It is only by risking our persons from one hour to another that we live at all. (Philosopher James Wilson on the advantages of sensation-seeking)

That said, sensation-seekers don't have the cleanest of track records. A high sensation-seeking score is a key factor in alcohol and smoking addiction. It's the personality pattern that most predicts early drug use. It's been implicated in sex addiction. Plus, high-sensation-seekers are more likely to have relationship problems and get divorced.

So if you know you're high on this pattern, you may want to slow down a bit. Yes, of course your gut reaction may be to think that living a low-sensation lifestyle means you'll be missing out (or copping out). But if you smoke and want to quit, if you take drugs and want to come off, if you push yourself from one crisis to another and want to chill ... the resources on page 293 will help.

☆ PS: Crowd hysteria

Find yourself in a group and your sensation-seeking bias may alter – usually upwards. In other words, given the euphoria a group provides, you may find yourself more sensation-seeking than normal.

For big life events, use that to motivate you. Get a trusted group – friends or family – to support you to take useful risks, to approach that prospective partner, to apply for that scary promotion.

But be careful when it comes to pure risk-taking, the sort of thing that happens on a Saturday night with the benefit of alcohol. Then, a group may egg you on beyond your physical or emotional limits. So if you sense that's happening, leave the group for a while and slope off on your own. And only go ahead if the urge is still with you when you've sobered up and chilled out!

what makes people tick?

HOW PERSONALITY WORKS 2

Move through life and you hit different stages. Different periods. Different roles. You start work. You leave home. You get married. You have children. You get as far as you're going to get in your job. Your children leave home. You retire.

Each stage changes you, slowly. It changes what you believe about the world. It changes what you believe about yourself. It changes what you believe about your life. For example …

- **becoming an adult may make you confident, give you more self-esteem**
- **leaving home may allow you to indulge your more sensation-seeking side**
- **falling in love may make you more optimistic about the future**
- **having children may make you more proactive – in order to cope**

In short, expect your personality to change as time passes. Plus, expect your partner's personality to change. And that of your friends, your children, your parents, your boss, your employees, the ticket collector on the number 73 bus …

The bottom line is this. If you have known someone for 5 years or through a time of crisis, two things are certain.

Their personality will have altered since you first met them.

And your personality will have altered since they first met you.

A sense of importance: sensory bias

6 Most of us have the use of five senses. Sight, sound, feeling, smell, taste. And for most of us, sight, sound and feeling – visual, auditory and kinaesthetic – are the crucial ones. Day to day, we tap into all three senses – and the three may be pretty well balanced. But there will be some priority order, a way in which we're more aware of one. Then another. Then another.

This sense bias will affect our whole personality. Do we learn best by looking at a book, listening to a tape, getting hands-on experience? Do we get turned on by someone's visual style, the sound of their voice, the way they feel?

Want to know your own sensory style? See page 262.

Our bias will affect what we're good at. Yes, people who are biased to sight do make better designers and people who are biased to sound do make better call-centre employees. And our bias will affect what we're bad at. The worst haircut in the history was probably from a stylist who managed to wander into hairdressing with no visual bias. The worst sex ever was probably with a lover who had 'nul points' on the kinaesthetic scale.

Visual bias

The way things look is what fascinates us. We have an eye for decor, we take a good photo, we love colour and shape and style. We're the ones who throw together superb clothes' mixes from the charity shop, while other lesser mortals buy pre-coordinated and still get it wrong. A visually-biased photographer friend of mine bounced herself back from depression by painting her lounge stunning shades of red and yellow. It not only transformed her house, it transformed her life.

Auditory bias

We have a bias to sound and we have an auditory talent – for sound, music, voices, accents. We're the ones who really can appreciate the sound system with the extra four noughts on the end of the price. The most auditory man I know found it literally hurt him to go into a shop that was playing music or to hear someone talking with a nasal twang.

Kinaesthetic bias

Those with a bias to the kinaesthetic love feeling on the outside – shape, texture, temperature and all things tactile. We'll snuggle into soft sweaters, luxuriate on velvet cushions, love getting – and giving – a touch, a hug, a massage. We're the ones who need to do something hands-on before we can understand it, the ones who need to test things out physically, for ourselves, before we can really approve them.

Expanding your bias

 When it comes to sensory bias, the ideal is a good spread. If you're low on one – not noticing it, not appreciating it – you're missing out on up to a third of life's goodies.

So how can you develop the sensory area you're lowest in? Simple – expose yourself to more experience of it. That will gradually make you more knowledgeable about – and therefore more appreciative of – that sense.

what makes people tick?

So do some things you would never normally do. Try some activities you would never normally try. Or go on courses. Join clubs. Plus, hang out with people who are strong in the sensory biases you're weak in – then practise what they preach.

- To get more visual bias in your life: get a visually-biased friend to show you how they put their 'look' together; join a painting or drawing class; take an art appreciation course; go to see visually stunning films – on a cinema screen, in all their glory ...
- To get more auditory bias in your life: ask an auditory-biased friend to play you music they like and explain why they like it; go to gigs, operas, concerts; tune the car radio to a music channel for the next few weeks; take singing lessons or voice training ...
- To get more kinaesthetic bias in your life: take a kinaesthetically-biased lover and let them teach you the joys of sensuous touch; get a regular massage, take a massage course; take dancing lessons, particularly if it involves moving with a partner; go to acting classes and explore 'internal feelings' – that is, your emotions ...

When you teach

Question: if you're dealing with other people, when does knowing about this personality pattern come in useful?

Basic answer: any time. It will always help you to know what sense someone prefers, because it helps you understand how they operate.

More subtle answer: any time you're presenting information to someone. For instance, when you're teaching. Or showing. Or explaining. Or demonstrating. Or motivating. Yes, of course when you're doing these things you'll include elements from all three senses – show, tell, hands-on. But you'll get further if you discover which sense a person is biased towards and major on that.

First, how do you discover their bias. You can use all the tips in section 21 of this book on reading other people. Or, quite simply, you can ask.

- 'Do you prefer me to explain this or to write it down?' – the answer will tell you whether someone is auditory-biased or visually-biased.
- 'Do you want me to let you have a go yourself?' – the answer will give you a lead on whether they have any kinaesthetic bias or not.

If someone is more visually-biased, take a visual approach. Use diagrams/charts. Write it up on a flip chart, let them take notes, give handouts at the end. Get out the map, draw them a picture, take them there and show them. And use visual words to focus the message and check that it's clear to them: 'do you see my point, does it look good, does that shed any light on it?' ...

If someone is biased more to auditory, then tell, explain, let them ask questions. Let them do it to music, give them a tape to take home. And use auditory words to tune in to the message and check they've really listened: 'does that ring a bell with you, can you hear what I'm saying, are we singing from the same hymn sheet?' ...

If someone is more kinaesthetically-biased, get them working in three dimensions and hands-on. Provide a model. Let them play and practise. Get them moving rather than just sitting still. And use kinaesthetic words to hammer home the message and check they've grasped it: 'does that feel OK, what's your gut reaction, can you get a handle on this?' ...

PS: Perfect presents

When present buying, your recipient's sensory bias can help you make a better purchase.

Think about what they already own. What characterizes the clothes they wear or the CDs they play or the crockery they use? What is it about these things – in terms of visual, auditory and kinaesthetic – that they value? The simple clean look? The rich tone? The snuggly feel?

Then go in search of presents that reflect these values – quite simply, the visual, auditory or kinaesthetic style that your recipient rates.

Tick-tock: time strategy

7 When it comes to experiencing time, there must be as many different ways as there are people in the world. But according to American anthropologist Edward T. Hall, there are two general subpatterns.

These ways of thinking about time are called 'time lines', because we imagine time as a line in our mental map.

One time line is termed 'in time', the other is called 'through time'.

How to find out which of the two 'time lines' you use

Take a moment now to get comfortable. Ideally, get a friend to talk you through the following instructions; if you're on your own, simply read and action each in turn.

- Think about something that happened to you when you were young – say about five years old. Now in what direction did you become aware of that memory – behind you, in front of you or to your left or right?
- Think of something that's going to happen in the future, a year or so ahead. Now in what direction did you become aware of that memory – behind you, in front of you or to your left or right?
- Now imagine a line joining the two points, the direction your past memory came from and the direction your future thought came from. You don't need to see the line clearly, just become generally aware of it.

- Finally, check where the line passes. Does it pass through your body? Or does it pass in front of you, so you don't have to turn your head to see it?

If any part of the time line passes through your body, then you're an in-time person. If the time line is all outside your body, then you're a through-time person.

In-time strategy

If we're an 'in-time' person, we see our timelines running into and out of our body. We see the past behind, the future ahead, the present mentally inside.

And that means we tend to see time from the inside rather than the outside – which means that we can be too involved to see it clearly. So however important time is to us, we'll tend to be vague about it, unsure how long things will take or how much time has passed.

I have an in-time friend who disappears off to the shops saying he'll be back in 20 minutes and turns up 4 hours later wondering what all the fuss is about. I've another in-time colleague who always lets meetings overrun and needs a flashcard for the word urgent. In-time people don't do deadlines.

In-time people, who keep their future in sight and put their past behind them, often prefer present and future.

On the other hand, in-time people do do peak experiences like no-one else. If we're 'in time', the present is likely to be vivid for us. We're living it, here and now, to the full. And, as time passes and an event becomes a memory, we may still recall it vividly because it's clear in our heads.

Conversely, when it comes to schedules, in-time people may not

In time.

Through time.

be able to remember or imagine *when* things happened, because we don't have an overall view of time as a whole. But on the plus side, that can mean that we are able to let the past go, put it behind us – which is where in-time people mentally put the past. Literally, no regrets.

It was millionaire Donald Trump who said, 'I try to learn from the past but I plan for the future by focusing exclusively on the present. That's where the fun is.' I'd lay heavy odds that Donald is an in-time person.

Through-time strategy

If we're a through-time person, we see our timelines all outside – often laid out in front of us. We'll probably see the past to the left, the future to the right (reversed if left-handed or from a culture where the written language flows from right to left). And our time-line is continuous, uninterrupted and whole. Which means that we can see it all; see how the bits interrelate.

what makes people tick?

With this sort of detailed mental diary available, most through-time people are sure of chronology. We can tell how long things are going to take. Our forward planning is excellent.

Past-oriented people are more likely to be through-time ... they can see their past, rather than having it behind them, out of view.

And we just love those ducky little time-management schemes that make our in-time colleagues scream because they haven't got the precise awareness of time that allows them to run the system happily. I have a through-time colleague who doesn't wear a watch – but who, when you want to know the time, hazards a guess to the nearest thirty seconds. And is always right.

Downsides of 'through time'? There's one. Through-time people have so much awareness of past and future that we can find it difficult to live in the moment. We're always remembering, planning or dreaming – and that can mean that present-time enjoyment is something we find hard to do.

When clocks collide

Say you're dealing with an off-the-scale in-time person. If it's their night to cook dinner, it could well be late. If it's their turn to chair a meeting, it's odds on things will overrun. How do you cope?

- Be patient with an in-timer's tendency to lateness. They rarely know what time it is or how long things take – so plan around that.
- Don't expect time management. They can't see the future clearly so they find it difficult to plan that – you may have to do this for them.
- Don't feel rejected if they lose concentration; they can find it

difficult to keep focused – so make explanations short and sweet.
- Appreciate their ability to live here and now – copy that and you'll live a more rewarding life.

Alternatively, what can you expect from an off-the-scale through-time person? If you have a difference of opinion, they remember it for years. If you send them identical birthday cards 10 years apart, they clock that. If they're organizing a project, they're completely anally retentive on deadlines. How do you cope?

- Be patient with a through-timer's obsession with punctuality. They feel bad if their life isn't scheduled – so respect that and be on track yourself.
- Don't expect them to forget things easily. Their lives are constantly before their eyes so they hang on to memories – you may have to live with that.
- Don't ask them to work in a noisy or chaotic environment. They can find it difficult to focus if there's mess around – so help them tidy up.
- Appreciate their ability to see time as a continuum – copy that and you'll live a more effective life.

An interesting variation

One of the cleverest jewellery adverts I've seen recently was for diamonds. It read: 'You feel in love ... you are in love ... you'll always be in love ... a diamond for your past, your present and your future'. It was clever because it appeals across the board ... to past people, present people and future people.

Because whether your time line is 'in time' or 'through time', you'll also have a time preference. Do you favour past? Present? Future? Which is more important to you? Which compels you?

If the past is more important ...

You love history and tradition. Either because you've seen a lot of it – older people may be more past-oriented than younger; or because you haven't seen enough of it – young countries may eulogize tradition more than those that have a longer history.

Or you just like hanging on to things and the past is something to hang on to. One of the most past-oriented people I know has not only kept every theatre programme back to 1972, she also keeps all her clothes – which considering how often fashion trends come round has served her well. She's currently pulling out the dark denim for the third time, though she's never, thankfully, resurrected the rara skirt!

To be able to look back upon one's past life with satisfaction is to live twice. (Past-oriented Roman writer Marcus Valerius Martial)

If you're a past-oriented person, you may have difficulty seeing the future and setting goals. So put effort into learning to think ahead and to create clear visions of what you want to see.

You may also have a problem letting go of the past or recovering from a past trauma. If this happens to you and you want to move on and start living in the present again, then counselling will almost always help. (See page 293 for further resources.)

If the present is more important ...

You'll tend to go for your peak experience now. You live for the moment, sliding off memories and not worrying about the future. You're often very spiritual or meditative or have had an illness, accident or near death experience which has made you glad to be alive.

Truly present-oriented people are rare – I've only ever met one. I'd known her for 3 years before I discovered she'd once been married – because she never refers to her past. And as to the future, she simply announces something is underway – house move, job move, new car – rather than tell you ahead of time. For her, nothing's truly real unless it's happening, right now.

Live each day the fullest you can, not guaranteeing ... tomorrow, not dwelling ... on yesterday. (Present-oriented actress Jane Seymour)

If you're present oriented, you'll benefit from more awareness of past and future. Make an effort to look backwards and forwards, to recall your early life, to create dreams. If this is difficult for you – perhaps because a trauma has made you block off certain feelings – then as with a past-oriented person, it may help to go to counselling. (See page 293 for further resources.)

If the future is more important ...

You always look ahead. You may do it temporarily because you're having a miserable here and now. Or you may do it permanently – and if so, you may be a kind of visionary, unrealistic and dreamy.

You may also, as a future-oriented person, view the past as utterly irrelevant. My husband is heavily future oriented and can literally forget what has happened an hour before. Many a time I've been mulling over the gory details of a row we've had, only to find that he's deleted it from his memory banks – a neat trick, which I constantly aim to emulate.

My interest is in the future – I'm going to spend the rest of my life there. (Future-oriented inventor Charles F. Kettering)

If you're a future-oriented person, you can end up living your life from one goal to the other, constantly putting off the here and now. Delayed gratification may become a way of life for you – because

what makes people tick?

you actively feel uncomfortable or guilty at enjoying the moment when you could be looking forward and getting things done.

But there is value in taking your eye off the future ball; the present and the past have lessons to offer that are useful for your hopes and dreams. So look around and look back – it will make your experience of the future more fulfilling.

Time for work?

Two of my colleagues – both business trainers – often work as a **$** team. They're good together. And one of the things that makes them so good together is that they have completely different time strategies.

So in the beginning, they see the client together, take a brief, chat it through on the way home. Thereafter Lisa – a through-time woman – plans the course and prepares the written material from a database. She finds it easy to tell how the training will run, because she can literally 'see' it in front of her. So she easily puts a timing on everything and prepares a variety of exercises and training material to cover every eventuality.

On the day, Kate – a classic in-time person – takes the lead. She's a past mistress at thinking on her feet, coping with what's happening in the here and now, batting whatever comes her way.

Of course, she couldn't have matched Lisa's meticulous precourse planning. Just as Lisa couldn't do the instant reactions that the training room demands. But working together, their courses always run like proverbial clockwork – before, during and after.

This is a classic example of how most work situations need both in-time and through-time people – but generally in different roles.

If you're a strong in-time person ...

- you'll be great in active, slightly hectic jobs, like nursing, reception work, marketing, mental health – where you're usually being asked to respond in the present, here and now. You may be a bit lax on your timesheets, but that will be more than made up for by your ability to come up with the goods on the spur of the moment.

If you're a strongly through-time person ...

- you'll be best at jobs that need an awareness of chronology – administrator, accountant, conference organizer. Plus, if you prefer the future, then planning and goal-setting will be your forte; if you prefer the past, then anything that involves checking, auditing or reviewing will play to your strengths.

PS: Instant diagnosis 2

To find out if someone is an in-time or through-time person, watch their hand movements.

Someone who's in-time will gesture back for the past and forward for the future. Someone who's through-time will gesture to one side (usually left) for the past and the other side (usually right) for the future.

I once dealt, over the phone, with a colleague whose ability to think on her feet convinced me she was in-time. And during our first face-to-face, I watched spellbound as she gestured in front of her when talking about a coming deadline and behind her when talking about last Christmas. Case proved!

what makes people tick?

Woods or trees:
big-picture/detail strategy

8 When we're taking in information – listening to a story, reading a report, hearing the latest gossip – we each have a best way of doing it, a way that feels easier and more natural to us, a way that lets us grasp the information more quickly and more elegantly.

We may go for the big picture – then imagine the details for ourselves. Or we may need to collect the details – then build the picture in our minds.

Big picture first, then detail

If we prefer big picture before detail, we start with and concentrate on the central idea. Only once we've got that, can we fit the jigsaw pieces into place. We map things out in general before we start thinking particulars, we make decisions on principle before considering the finer points.

Want to know your own strategy? See page 264.

Often, we won't actually be interested in the specifics much at all – like Albert Einstein, we'll be prone to muttering, 'I want to know God's thoughts – the rest are details'. But abstracts, ideas, goals, concepts, visions – those really turn us on. As will long-term plans, year by year rather than day by day. We got very excited at the thought of the Millennium – but have trouble with what's happening after lunch.

This can be frustrating for people around us, who need us to act on details just occasionally – like putting the cat out, ordering the milk, filling in that time sheet or remembering it's their birthday!

Detail first, then big picture

If we prefer details first and then the big picture, we start with the specifics and, from that, deduce what the framework is. Tell us what each of the jigsaw pieces are and we'll generalize out to the central concept. Tell us about seven thousand five hundred and forty-two trees and we'll conclude there's a wood.

Or give us a list, schedule, catalogue, box of buttons or pile of pages and we're fine, because detail-oriented people just love reorganizing, cross-referencing so that all the little bits fall into place. They just love telling the story element by sequential element.

There's only one drawback to being a detail-oriented person – a really big picture may scare us as just too huge. We'll get confused, unhappy or simply uninterested in anything truly abstract, anything that seems impossible to consider in small sections, like 'double the sales figures.' We need to break projects like these down into a point-by-point plan before we can take action.

As the old joke goes, give us an elephant and we'll eat it – but we'll eat it one bite at a time.

15% of people like detail first, then big picture, 60% of people like big picture first, then detail, 25% of people vary

Here's an example

To sum it all up, here's how a detail-oriented person and a big-picture person go about cooking. (I know. I used to share a flat with one of each.)

The detail-oriented person sits down at the start of each week, plans her menus for each evening, lists out the ingredients she needs, checks off whether she's got them, then goes round the supermarket ticking off each one as she buys it. Every evening she looks at the relevant recipe, pulls out the exact appropriate ingredients and cooks the meal.

what makes people tick?

A big-picture person bulk-buys brown rice, nuts, beans and sauces every three months at the local health food store. Every week, he looks at what he's got, generates a one-pot meal from it and keeps it boiling through the week. Done and dusted.

Getting both wood and trees

Rolling Stones lead singer Mick Jagger – not only one of the world's greatest rock stars, but also a stunningly wealthy business-man – on being asked what lay behind his success replied, 'You need an eye for detail ... but you mustn't lose sight of the big picture you had originally.' Exactly, Mick.

In short, like Jagger, most effective personalities are happy with both big picture and details, with both abstract concepts and specifics. Because such people can move easily from one to the other – and back again.

So if you think that you're biased towards one end of the scale, then take action. Get more of a spread.

If you're more big-picture-oriented, learn the detail-oriented way

- Detail-oriented people get a visceral thrill from crossing off each job done; hence their love of lots of tiny jobs! Learn that skill by listing each small part of a task, then making a big issue of noting it's done, with a stabilo, gold pen, erasing scribble or whatever delivers a feelgood factor.
- Detail people prioritize the enjoyable parts of any job. So they get loads of stuff cleared happily and face what's left knowing the job's well underway. So don't force yourself to tackle the hardest bits of a project first. Begin by doing the bits you enjoy – to get up some speed for the harder parts.
- Detail people reward themselves constantly – not just every few

 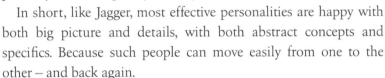

months, but every few minutes! So don't wait for the end of a task to celebrate, but give yourself regular celebrations – a cup of coffee, a walk round the block, a mental pat on the back – as you complete sections of a task.

If you're more detail-oriented, learn the big-picture way

- Big-picture people simplify things by taking decisions on principle. So if you have a key decision to make and listing the various pros and cons doesn't work, ask what single principle is at stake. What's moral? What's right? Find one fundamental principle to guide your decision and your glorious detail strategies will click into place to help you implement it.
- Big-picture people often choose between two options by imagining each as a single big-picture image. So if you have to choose, get two thoughts that represent the results of each choice. One will make you feel better than the other. Choose that one – then use your detail skills to make it work in practice.
- Big-picture people motivate themselves by focusing on the one most important aspect of a goal. So next time you have an aim in mind, allow yourself the luxury of simply imagining how good it's going to be, no question. Then let that motivate you to move forward.

Taking a brief

So you're taking a brief for something: from your boss who wants you to do a big project or from your partner who wants you to do the shopping. No matter what it is, if you want to do a good job – without giving yourself a bad time – be aware of big-picture and detail patterns.

This is vital because if the person briefing you is big-picture-oriented, you need to go about getting instructions from them in a particular way. If the person briefing you is detail-oriented, you need to get instructions from them in a completely different way. Tackle it wrong and you end up dazed and confused. (And so do they.)

With a big-picture-oriented briefer
- Get them first talking about what the overall goal is and get them enthusiastic about it. They'll find this easy – it's the bit they most enjoy. Get them to tell you in broad detail just how they'll know the job is complete, what you'll present to them, what they'll be happy with.
- Don't pin them down with details too early – talk in general terms about ideas, concepts. When you move into details, get your timing right – given too many specifics too early, big-picture people drown. So stop occasionally to summarize what's happening at a more global level.
- When you've done the job they're asking you to do, don't expect them to check every detail – they may have lost interest by then. So be prepared to do the detailed checking yourself.
- A big-picture person starts with only a general idea of what's wanted – so it may only be when you've taken the project forward that it becomes clear what's wrong on a detailed level. If so, keep calm and be prepared to correct further at this stage.
- A variation on this last point in the work context is that the briefer may approve your work, but then passes it down to a more detail-aware assistant who starts coming up with very specific criticisms. Again, don't panic. Just shift strategies and approach this new person as detail-oriented – because almost certainly they will be.

With a detail-oriented briefer
- Get them first talking about precisely how they see the end product and get them enthusiastic about it. You may get thrown

as they bombard you with details, descriptions and examples. But hang in there – they need to do this in order to get clarity for themselves.

- Once they've explained everything, then is the time to go back and summarize it for them – and for you – to make sure you have really understood what they're saying.
- Watch out for detail-oriented briefers overcontrolling the tiniest elements, and wanting to take charge. Don't balk – simply list out what you're doing, get their approval for the process, then identify three or four key stages at which you'll report back to let them check your work. That will keep them happy – and keep them off your back.

One small step for man, one giant leap for mankind (Neil Armstrong's historic quote for the Apollo moon landing was details first, then big picture)

As an even better option, you can simply let your detail-orientated briefer do your job for you – because given half a chance, they will.

One woman copywriter I know has a client with a serious detail pattern. When he rings her to commission a piece of writing, he knows precisely and specifically what he wants; so she simply takes notes on everything he says, in the order he says it. She then rings off, types up her notes, adds a stunning first and last paragraph and emails it back.

The client is happy because he's got exactly what he had in mind.

My colleague is happy because, basically, she's been paid a nice fat fee for taking dictation.

what makes people tick?

Which job?

Most careers mix big picture and detail. You do the filing (detail), **$** write some letters (mixture), plan a project (big picture). And so long as you aren't off-the-scale one way or the other, most jobs will suit you. You'll be able to move between the specifics and the more global thinking that's demanded of you.

But if you're highly detail-oriented – find it difficult to ever get your head round the big picture – you'll need to land a job where you can deal with lots of separate elements and get a buzz from crossing them off your list every day. Think call centre work or invoice inputting.

If you're highly big-picture-oriented and find it difficult to ever get your head round the details, then you'll need to land a job involving big thinking, policy, strategy or overall direction. I heard of one franchise chain – in need of big-picture leaders – who had a manager-entry application form that began 'How do you want to be remembered when you die?' Nice one. No-one who could only do detailed thinking would get beyond that incredibly big-picture question.

Finally, don't fall into the trap of thinking that in order to do a creative job, you need a big-picture personality. Sure, we tend to think of artists or writers as having big, big ideas. But creative thinking often starts with details. Writer Jane Austen likened her writing talent to the ability to paint with a fine brush on a two-inch-wide piece of ivory. Artist Vincent Van Gogh once said that 'Great things are done by a series of small things brought together.'

So if you're a detail person, don't think you can't be creative. After all, if detail is good enough for Austen and Van Gogh, it's good enough for you!

What's your magic number?

Here's an interesting variation on big-picture and detail thinking.

When we organize our thoughts, we usually divide them into sets. If you're a big-picture thinker, you'll tend to divide things into a small number of sets – be comfortable with only a few mental elements. If you're a detail-oriented thinker you'll tend to divide things into a large number of sets – be comfortable with a large number of mental elements.

The number you're most comfortable with is known (in my particular branch of psychology) as your 'magic number'.

Your magic number influences the way you operate. My husband has the magic number three. He not only likes to give three examples whenever he's talking through a point. He also organizes every project he starts so that it has three sections. He argues that two tends to create conflict, while four is 'somehow' too many. Of course it's too many. For him.

Conversely, I've a colleague who's heavily detail-oriented. Fifty things on her tick list – easy peasy. A hundred things to check – no problem. Her big-picture-oriented colleagues end up weeping on the floor as she gives her seventy-first example to prove her point. She's just getting up to speed.

Because people's magic numbers differ so much, there is in fact a problem. In short, you can feel uncomfortable with someone else's and they can feel uncomfortable with yours. Say your magic number is two and theirs is twenty-two. You'll feel overwhelmed because they give far too many examples and you get confused. They'll feel underwhelmed because you never give them enough examples and they get bewildered.

So spot other people's magic numbers. The quickest way is to ask them to explain something and watch for the number of examples they give. Often they'll mark out each point with a hand gesture, so you can count the movements as well as listening to the words. (If they make so many tiny movements that you lose count, they have a very high magic number indeed.)

Once you know what someone's magic number is, work with it. If someone's got a small number, make just a few broad points and don't offer too many details or illustrations. If they have a large magic number, expect to give lots of specifics and examples before you see the light begin to dawn.

PS: Storytelling tip 1

Whether you're telling a bedtime story to an under five or giving a business anecdote to a room full of MDs, start by framesetting in a general way to keep the big-picture people happy: 'Once upon a time, in a land far away …'

Then quickly move to examples to reel in the detail-oriented people. 'There was a little girl who lived in a wood. She had two tiny white kittens who had eyes bluer than the sea.' If the listeners faze out on the specifics, move back to more general stuff. If they hang in there with the specifics, carry on with the story detail by detail.

For closure, go back to the big picture: 'And they lived happily ever after …'

Equilibrium or metamorphosis: sameness/difference strategy

9 We all need some stability in life, in order to feel safe and secure. And we all need some change in life, in order to remain interested and engaged. But most of us have a preference within our personality for one or the other.

Want to know your own strategy? See page 265.

So we notice what's similar or we register what's different. We feel happier if there's stability – or more euphoric if there's some variety. We get uncomfortable when things change – or restless when they stay the same.

More sameness

If we favour sameness, we're far more likely to notice what's similar, what matches, what fits. Mentally, what we do is to look back and see what's happened before – and go for that again because we know it works. So we go to that same hotel year after year. We like classic clothes. We hang out with the crowd we've known since college. When we sign up for an evening course in September, our idea of a drastic shift in direction is to take the intermediate class where before we took beginners.

And because of this, long term, we feel uneasy with change. There's no place like home – preferably the same home we've lived in for decades. We'll hesitate before switching jobs. We'll find it difficult to adapt if a long-term relationship comes to an end.

what makes people tick?

More difference

If we favour difference, we're far more likely to notice what's different, new, alternative. What we hate is what came before, what's old, what's the same. Our motto is Mae West's: 'When choosing between two evils, I always like to try the one I've never tried before.'

We're the person who goes to a new club every Friday night, follows fashion, buys gadgets. When we sign up for an evening course, we take a different subject every time – and only ever commit for a term so we have a chance to shift class again after Christmas.

And because of this, long term, variety is our spice of life. So we may feel trapped if a relationship lasts more than a few months. We may get restless once we've settled into a new flat. Or we may be

like a colleague of mine who so loved job variety that she decided to go temping. But she did it permanently. Ten years and 52 jobs later, she says she's just about ready to take a permanent post. My bet is that she'll last about a year – and then want to move on.

Be careful not to confuse difference orientation with sensation-seeking (page 50). Yes, some sensation-seekers do go for novelty – but many don't like it; they go for the same kinds of risk over and over again. And yes, many difference-oriented people want high stimulation – but many fight shy of true sensation-seeking as far too dangerous!

Context

In general, most people want some sameness with a little difference – in other words, life stability with a few bits of variety thrown in. Too much of the old and people get bored. Too much of the new and they get insecure.

Plus, everyone differs depending on the context. So a person may be difference-oriented in clothes, sameness-oriented in shoes – they buy a new outfit every week but wear the same pair of comfortable sandals every day. Someone may be sameness-oriented in jobs, difference-oriented in relationships – they stay with their firm 30 years but get through five marriages.

And this pattern can be very mood-influenced. One of my colleagues has a highly difference-oriented approach to life. But when he's tired and stressed, his love of sameness leaps to the fore. His wife reports that on holiday, he always wants to go to new restaurants and sample untried cuisine. But at the end of a long hard week at work, a nice familiar TV dinner is about as different as he can handle.

Equally, someone who is difference-oriented may switch to sameness over the course of their lifetime. A classic trigger is having children. Pre-family life, you loved novelty and variety.

what makes people tick?

Enter three under-fives and suddenly you just want a bit of old familiar routine to stop you going round the bend because your life is so demanding.

Which is one reason why couples go clubbing and parents become couch potatoes!

Change, don't change!

Where difference and sameness mostly affects your interpersonal relationships is in your home life. OK, so a colleague, boss or employee likes novelty or stability. So what. You can walk away from it.

But if your sister, your flatmate – or particularly your partner – is on one extreme or the other here, then you'll know about it. You'll get the drama when they dump their well-paid job every 6 months – or the equal drama when they refuse to dump their career even though in your opinion it's decades past its sell-by date.

So it can work well to choose your friends and lovers with identical preferences for sameness or difference.

That was certainly what Gordon and Rita Turner have done. They have – apparently with no friction between them at all – moved 43 times in the past 47 years; the longest they've lived anywhere has been four years, the shortest one day. Quite simply, when it comes to houses, they share a difference-orientation of phenomenal proportions. Otherwise, the divorce would have loomed long ago.

But – unlike Gordon and Rita – you may well be attracted to someone who has a complementary rather than an identical approach. That's more than likely – because humans do follow the theory of 'opposites attract'. And then you have to work out ways of organizing your lives so that you don't drive each other mad.

Partner difference, you sameness

- Your partner likes novelty, hates routine, wants to do things differently every single day, loves switching jobs or houses or even countries.
- You end up feeling confused and insecure.
- Wherever possible, support their need for difference. There will be some things – say, holidays or redecorating – that actually won't wobble you at all. And if you can go along with your partner in these, they'll be far less restless, far less likely to hanker for the huge changes that threaten you.
- Build your own stability reminders. One sameness friend of mine had to travel to all sorts of odd places on business. In each new hotel she'd unpack from her case some family photos, a familiar CD and a snuggly rug to act as comfort blanket – home from home.

Partner sameness, you difference

- Your partner likes to keep things stable, prefers familiarity, feels uneasy if you suggest switching brands of breakfast cereal, let alone lifestyles.
- You end up feeling bored and blocked.
- Wherever possible, support your partner's need for sameness. Honour their routines and their rituals. In particular, build an atmosphere of emotional stability that makes them feel secure. If you can do this, they'll be far more able to keep up with the more varied lifestyle you want.
- Create difference in life areas where you operate alone. Opt for a varied career that keeps you interested. Take up new hobbies or go on a whole series of evening courses. Meet your need for difference in ways that don't threaten your home life.

Big changes

Here's a final suggestion if you want to make a biggish change in circumstances and know your partner will feel resistant. Do a trial run.

For example, my husband wanted to buy a black sports convertible but I'm massively sameness-oriented around cars and loved our old red saloon passionately. In fact, I'd always said that when it finally died a death, I'd replace it with an identical one, just a few years newer.

How on earth did my husband bridge the gap between our needs? Simple. He asked me to try the new car for four weeks – without selling the old one – and promised that if after that I didn't like it, he'd cancel the lease.

Of course, four weeks later, the new car had become the norm. I was used to it. I now love it with a passion and swear that when it finally dies a death, I'll replace it with an identical one, just a few years newer!

If you want your sameness-oriented partner (or your boss, manager or employee) to change something, ask them to try out that change for a limited period. And promise them, genuinely, that if they're not happy after the trial run, they can change back. Almost always, once they have changed, they'll stick to what they have now grown to know and love.

If you're off-the-scale sameness-oriented, you typically stay in a job 15–20 years and only leave if the company changes and makes you feel uncomfortable.

The daily grind

If you prefer sameness, you'll want a job with stability: the same $ kind of role from year to year, a reliable group of people around you.

In some ways, you're an employer's dream because you don't get restless and want to move onward or upward. You'll be the stable one, the solid one, the one they can rely on.

Unless, of course, an employer needs flexibility, in which case you're their nightmare. Because if they alter something, you'll feel uneasy. If they ask you to take on new responsibility, you'll throw a wobbly. You'll find it difficult to switch hats, do new projects, adapt to a change of direction or management.

If you're sameness-oriented with just a little liking for difference, you typically change jobs every 5–7 years.

So if you're heavily sameness-oriented, choose a post that stays stable, within a company on a low growth curve, where you can hunker down and do what you're best at – keeping things the same. Or if things do alter, then chill out by reminding yourself of the existing skills you're calling on or the similarities there are to your old role.

That said, the world today often doesn't value 'sameness' people. You're expected to like a job with variety, to move posts every few years for promotion. And so it's usually good to have at least some difference orientation.

If you're difference-oriented with just a little liking for sameness, you typically move jobs every 2–3 years.

What if you're heavily difference-oriented? Then, you need a job where things are never the same from day to day – like news journalism, nursing, consultancy or the armed forces. And unlike your sameness-oriented colleagues, you'll be happy working in a profession or company that is on a rapid growth curve or on a path of change, change, change.

what makes people tick?

If you're off-the-scale difference-oriented, you typically get restless and move every six months, even if you like your job.

Equally, if you're heavily difference-oriented, you'll want to shine in the jobs you do, to grab the attention by your unique style, echoing George Washington's belief that 'if you do the common things in life in an uncommon way, you will command the attention of the world.'

Watch out, countersorter about

There's an interesting little variation on difference orientation. It's called 'countersorting'. And it severely wobbles all kinds of relationships.

Countersorting means always sorting through things to find what's counter, or different. In other words, a countersorter thinks different always and everywhere. So someone says that a project ought to be given out to a freelance contractor – and the countersorter offers that it ought to be done in-house. Fair enough.

But if someone then agrees that yes, keeping the job in-house is an excellent idea, the countersorter will automatically begin arguing that it's best done by a freelancer, no question.

And if the argument somehow switches back round to the countersorter's point of view, they'll flip over once again – without malice aforethought – and take a different tack.

Notice I said 'without malice aforethought'. We're not talking viciousness here. Or a desire to prove a point. Or even a desire to act on the alternatives that the countersorter insists on thinking up. What we're talking is a spontaneous fascination with those alternatives. A countersorter loves to find what's different in any situation. And because of that, they change their mind several times a minute. The effect on other people can best be described as 'interesting'.

Now, other countersorters don't even notice what's happening because they're too busy countersorting themselves.

But sameness-oriented people find themselves screwed into the ground on a right-hand twist because whatever they say, the countersorter will point out ways in which things are different. Of course, the 'sameness' person will shift in an attempt to get the consensus and agreement they feel comfortable with. Upon which, the countersorter will shift again in a different direction.

This is challenging enough in a work or social context. Add love to the mixture and you can have real problems. The sameness partner wants just a few occasions where their lover agrees with them. The countersorter partner wants the freedom to keep exploring different ideas. Is there a way out before they each start gazing wistfully at the nearest bread knife?

Three coping mechanisms for handling a countersorter

- Give a countersorter time to explore their thoughts fully rather than rushing in and arguing the point – you'll find they'll have more space and willingness to consider your suggestions.
- Keep clearly in mind, even under provocation, that countersorting isn't motivated by a need to hurt, but by a need to get the buzz of difference. (If the countersorter is motivated to hurt, then this isn't true countersorting, it's mental abuse. Get it sorted.)
- Realize that when a countersorter disagrees, their agenda isn't to rule out your suggestion, it's to explore all possible ideas. So when they're done exploring, repeat your original thought; they just might take you up on it.

Three coping mechanisms if you're a countersorter

- When someone suggests something, acknowledge it before moving on to exploring different options. Use phrases like 'that's interesting, good idea'. Start using the word 'and' rather than 'but', as in 'I like that thought and I want to add ...'.

- If anyone else has an idea, reassure them that, in the end, you will consider it – you just need to explore a few ideas of your own first. And, when you have explored, make sure to go back and consider the other person's suggestion.
- If you notice anyone getting edgy or irritable when you're busy considering possibilities, back off and allow them to cool down. You're probably countersorting in a way that upsets them. Do some soothing and you'll be able to carry on exploring ideas without hassle.

PS: Perfect holidays

Sameness-oriented people own a holiday cottage and go there every year for the same two weeks. Difference-oriented people ski in the winter, sunbathe in summer and take city breaks spring and fall.

So if you and a holiday companion argue, mix and match. Go for the same activity but a new place – sightseeing in Venice, then Toronto, then Cape Town.

Or choose similar venues but with different activities – like one of those 'Club' holidays, upmarket holiday camps where the deal is comfortingly standard across every resort in the world, but with up to 65 different activities to choose from and a different cabaret every night.

Trust but verify: believing style

10 Every day, we take several leaps of faith. We buy fruit without tasting it, are convinced by a colleague's argument, believe what a friend tells us, agree to a partner's suggestion ... in general, take a hundred and one things on trust.

But how do we start to believe, how do we get convinced – and how do we know when to hold back and reserve judgement? There are three distinct components involved in this personality pattern.

Credible medium

Want to know your own strategy? See page 266.

To believe, we need evidence. And the medium through which we get it is crucial. The majority of us rely most on what we see and, after that, on verbal evidence. (That's why TV ads, where a picture and a voice combine to make a point, are particularly effective.)

- *Written evidence*: we credit something if we read it – a report, newspaper article, letter of recommendation; we need to literally see things 'in black and white'. Three per cent of people have this subpattern.
- *Verbal evidence*: we value something if someone else said it; we need to hear it 'through the grapevine'. Thirty per cent of people have this subpattern.
- *Visual evidence*: we're convinced by watching – a demonstration, diagrams, pictures, graphs; for us, 'seeing is believing'. Fifty-five per cent of people have this subpattern.

what makes people tick?

- *Hands-on evidence*: we need to experience something before we believe in it. We have to see the performance, test the car; for us, 'the proof of the pudding is in the eating'. Twelve per cent of people have this subpattern.

Credible source

If we're going to believe, we also need to believe in whoever – or whatever – is offering the evidence.

- *Own judgement*: we make a judgement only on our own perceptions, thoughts and feelings; we're likely to doubt all other forms of evidence.
- *Objective proof*: we want evidence presented from some objective source like a consumer magazine or a research study; we've no need for the experience so long as we see the statistics.
- *A trusted friend*: we want a word-of-mouth recommendation from someone we know personally; we trust them.
- *A credible role model:* we need someone in authority or with expertise to tell us something's true; this doesn't have to be in person – a quote or a TV appearance will do.

Repetition

Repetition convinces – but how much repetition of the evidence do we need before we can believe in something?

- *With repetition*: we believe something if it's repeated often enough; the number of times it needs repeating will vary with context. Fifty-two per cent of people have this subpattern.
- *Almost never*: we're hardly ever convinced; but if we do tip over, then of course we'll hardly ever tip back and become unconvinced. Fifteen per cent of people have this subpattern.

- *Automatic*: we accept something immediately, on just a small amount of information and no repetition at all. Eight per cent have this subpattern.

Mix and match

Credible medium, credible source, repetition ... there are endless variations in believing style. So everyone's particular combination of components will be utterly unique to them.

So at work, a project manager may see some figures just once and be convinced that a tender is viable; he needs 'visual evidence', he needs an 'objective source' and he needs them 'automatically'. His colleague, on the other hand, may need to hear feedback and opinion from several consultants in order to feel the same – she needs 'verbal evidence', 'a trusted friend' and 'with repetition'.

And when it comes to romance ... as an agony aunt, I hear countless stories of how people become convinced about a partner – in other words, how they fall in love. And boy, does it vary! I've known 'written evidence' people swept off their feet by erotic emails. I've known 'trusted friend' people needing a thumbs up from parents or mates. I've known 'almost never' men wobbling for years about marriage – but who, once committed, remain so for life.

'Trust. But verify.' (An old Russian proverb, obviously thought up by someone with an 'objective proof' pattern)

Finally, here's a story which neatly illustrates all believing style components brought into play. In 1938, in the United States, a radio dramatization of H. G. Wells' *The War of the Worlds* was broadcast live. It caused nationwide panic. People were screaming in the streets because they were genuinely convinced that Earth was being invaded by aliens.

what makes people tick?

Why did everyone fall for it? First, because the credible medium was convincing – the dramatization sounded like a news alert. Second, because the credible source was convincing – the public believed that the radio never lied. Third, because the public 'automatically' believed – the possibility of an alien invasion was something so horrifying that they didn't bother to check it out; they bought into it immediately!

There's a moral here. Because the bottom line is that when it comes to believing, emotion rules. So if we want something enough, we'll ignore the proof that it's dangerous. And if we fear something enough, then we'll ignore the proof that it's safe.

The War of the Worlds' audience was so panicked by the programme, they didn't even register the weighty evidence that the whole thing was fiction!

No more buyer's remorse

Do you get buyer's remorse? Do you eagerly get your hands on a new dress or a new job, eagerly wash your hands of an old car or an old lover – then spend endless regretful nights? If so, this bit is for you. Because you can learn to improve your decision-making ability – by looking at just where your believing style leads you astray.

Wrong credible medium

If you only rely on only one kind of evidence to make a decision, you'll make the wrong decision. There are four different sorts of proof that you can gather – written, verbal, visual, hands on. Get at least two for every choice or decision you make. So don't just look at the shoes in the window – try them on. Don't just rely on a handshake to seal the deal – get it in writing too.

Wrong credible source

Objective sources may seem undeniable. Until you remember that tobacco companies have spent the last century or so producing 'objective evidence' that cigarettes don't harm you. So check out any evidence you're tempted to believe; with research in particular, try to find out if there are other studies that contradict the one you're being convinced by.

A person who runs 'own judgement' style tends to be internally-inspired (page 151).

And, when it comes to people, sad though it seems, some folk are always suspect. Because if someone tells you something, they've almost certainly got a vested interest in your believing it. And the bigger the reward they get for telling you, the bigger the vested interest they've got.

Plus, don't believe anyone just because they look convincing – get evidence of their trustworthiness. And even then, don't believe everything you hear. British peer-turned-convict Jeffrey Archer has claimed to have three A Levels, a degree from Oxford and to have spent a year at Sandhurst Military College. (He actually has three O levels, a one-year teaching diploma at Oxford and no Sandhurst experience whatsoever.)

what makes people tick?

Not enough repetition

Once is not enough for most major decisions. Test-drive more than one car. Look round more than one house. Try on that bank-breaking dress a second time, on another day.

When I'm interviewing for a job, I always get the top candidates back for a second interview a few days after the first round. And always – every single time – the impression that candidates make on me is slightly different on the second interview from the first. The impressive candidate on initial viewing isn't always the best candidate on a second viewing. The nervous candidate first time round may shine when given another chance.

A person who runs 'a trusted friend' style tends to be externally-inspired (page 151).

Too much emotion

If something feels good (or bad), then it's sensible to take that feeling into account. But if something feels very, very, very good or very, very bad, then we often see that as proof positive that it's right for us or wrong for us. But in fact, the world doesn't work like that.

'Hello, I love you. Won't you tell me your name?' is highly arousing, but, on its own, not the way to make a good long-term decision like getting married or getting pregnant. 'We just think you're soooo right for this role' is supremely flattering, but, on its own, not the basis of a good long-term decision like taking a job.

A person who runs 'a credible role model' style will tend to be externally-inspired (page 151).

So if you feel strongly emotional about something, always double-check. Someone outside the situation, without your emotional vulnerability, will calm you down and provide an objective viewpoint.

Sure, it's tempting to go for what you feel strongly about – but if something's meant to be, then it will survive a second opinion. If it doesn't survive, it wasn't a good idea in the first place.

Getting that raise

$ You want your boss to give you a pay increase. Or more holiday or better perks or a promotion … or whatever. How do you persuade her (or him)? Simply, meet all her believing style criteria – then you'll have a much better chance of getting what you want.

So check out your boss's believing style. What do you know of her? What do you know about how she makes decisions in general and decisions about pay in particular? What's happened other times you've asked for an increase? What's happened when other people have asked for an increase? Then, once you've identified her style, tailor your request to fit her needs.

What credible medium does your boss need?
- *Written evidence, verbal evidence, visual evidence, hands-on evidence*. How does your boss like to see requests presented – on paper, a verbal presentation by you or only material she gathers herself? Adapt your approach to what she prefers – perhaps some paper evidence plus a follow-up face-to-face discussion.

Which credible source does your boss believe?
- *Her own judgement*: your boss needs to know that she herself feels you deserve an increase. This is a tough one – you may never get what you ask for if she hasn't already independently decided that you should have it.
- *Objective proof*: your boss needs to be able to measure that you're worth it. Go in with evidence of your extra responsibilities or increased output.
- *The marketplace*: she needs to know that other people in your situation are earning the salary you're asking for. Get hold of industry figures from employment agencies.
- *Peers*: she needs to know that respected other people in her field

          what makes people tick?

are giving their employees the rate you want. Collect job ads showing salaries offered by known competitors.

- *Company policy*: she needs to know that the firm itself will approve of her decision. Do your homework and show that colleagues with the same track record, qualifications or experience as you are earning the salary you're after.
- *You:* she'll give you an increase just because you feel you need it. This one's not usual – it typically only happens in small companies. But if your boss does work on this assumption, you've got it made. Just don't lower your credibility by asking for a rise too often!

What amount of repetition does your boss need?

- *With repetition*: your boss needs the request repeating. This doesn't mean constantly talking about a pay increase; it does mean creating a number of opportunities to present different pieces of persuasive proof. Only push for a decision after two or three mentions, meetings or presentations.
- *Almost never*: your boss hardly ever agrees to a suggestion. Put the ball in her court, asking what she'd need to see you do, the ways in which you would need to change, in order for her to agree to the raise. Then fulfil her requirements and present her with the evidence that you've done it.
- *Automatic:* your boss will be convinced immediately or not at all. So if she says no to your request, don't ask again until you have new arguments or evidence. If she says yes, expect her to monitor your progress – automatics make their decisions instantly, but check those decisions thoroughly.

What kind of emotional charge does your boss need?

In a work context, people are usually very suspicious of emotions. If they feel emotional, they usually see that as a sign to stop and rethink a decision – or to back off making it at all.

So if you accompany your request for a raise by strong appeals or threats, your boss will probably see this as counter-evidence of your suitability for a pay increase. And then she'll probably refuse.

Cold sell

$ You're selling cold. By that I don't mean you're behind a shop counter in the middle of winter. I mean that you're trying to convince people you don't know to buy, believe or do something. But because you don't know them, you don't know their personalities. So how can you begin to tailor your sales pitch to their personality needs?

Here's how. There are some neat statistics that suggest that if you sell (or persuade or convince) in a particular way, then even if you haven't been able to get much advance knowledge at all about the personalities you're talking to, you've a good chance of reaching most of the people most of the time. Not all of the people all of the time. But enough.

This model is based on believing style – but it also pulls in some other personality patterns; I mention each as it becomes relevant.

- Outline your framework briefly before you begin. Sixty per cent of people like to be given an overview of what they're going to hear before they hear it (big picture/detail strategy page 71).
- Use visuals (preferably the item you're actually selling, but failing that, a picture of it) plus spoken words. Fifty-five per cent of people need to see something to believe it, but add in voice and that figure rises to nearly 100 per cent (sensory bias, page 57).
- Tell people the benefits of what you're selling, but also tell them what problems it helps them avoid. Most people are convinced if they get both the carrot and the stick (towards/away-from strategy, page 17).

what makes people tick?

- Tell people that what you're offering is more effective than what they already have. Fifty per cent of people want to be convinced that there's a better way (sameness/difference strategy, page 80).
- Don't stress novelty too much. Sixty-five per cent of people are happy with change so long as it's not too extreme (sameness/difference strategy, page 80).
- Do stress that by buying into this thing, people are part of a group. Remember that classic advertising slogan 'five billion VW owners can't be wrong'. Seventy-five per cent of people believe that everyone is similar – so inferring there's a trend means people are more likely to follow it (difference strategy, page 80).
- Finally, recap on the main points. Fifty-two per cent of people will believe anything if it's repeated often enough.

If the product (or suggestion or proposition or argument) is worthwhile, by this time it should be 'job's in the bag!'

PS: When automatic turns nasty

Trauma flips everyone into 'automatic' believing style.

A strongly negative experience – a car crash, mad dog, rape – can in a split second teach the recipient that the trigger – car, dog, rapist – is overwhelmingly and intrinsically threatening. They end up terrified to drive, see a dog on television, talk to someone new.

Such trauma isn't for amateurs to mess with. Get professional support to rework the original event and reverse the learning – the Resources section (page 293) gives suggestions.

HOW PERSONALITY WORKS 3

Life always has a new challenge for you, whether it's a good challenge (an exam success, a promotion, a lottery win, a new baby on the way) or a bad challenge (illness, redundancy, divorce, a bereavement).

Every one of these challenges will shift your personality – and not just emotionally or temporarily. A 1998 study shows that a key life event will actually alter your brain synapses. You change biologically when life impacts on you – your whole being shifts. For example:

- **If you're separated from your parents as a child, you may end up feeling a little wary of life, pessimistic about it.**
- **If you're bullied as a child or as an adult, you may end up resisting all attempts to convince you of something or constantly move 'away from' problems.**
- **A bereavement can switch your time focus from future hope to past regret – as can losing a job or losing a love.**
- **A huge success may build your self-esteem, make you more sure of yourself, more able to handle change.**

The lesson here is that if you – or someone you know – has a big crisis in life, then expect them to change as a result. The colleague who gets married, the spouse whose father dies, the friend who gets divorced, the neighbours who have a baby – these people's personalities will alter as a result of these events.

Personality isn't stable. It shifts according to what the world throws at you.

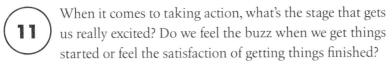

Setting the wheels in motion: starting/finishing strategy

11 When it comes to taking action, what's the stage that gets us really excited? Do we feel the buzz when we get things started or feel the satisfaction of getting things finished?

This personality pattern isn't just about starting and completing a specific task – it's much broader than that. Starting could mean generating ideas, stirring up energy, beginning a new relationship. Finishing could mean making a decision, getting a result or celebrating the completion of a big work project.

More starting

If we prefer starting, we'll get a real buzz at the beginning of things. We love having initial thoughts, setting things up, laying down the basics – that first enthusiastic energy is what gets us going.

There are a lot of us around, just think of the kit car craze – the idea that one buys a car in kit form, piece by piece, adding to it when one's got the time and energy to carry on. The manufacturers report that they sell lots of the starter kit, when people have the vision – but thereafter sales tail off very quickly. Hardly anyone ever completes the car.

Want to know your own strategy? See page 272.

Because for a starting person, the energy goes as soon as the initial stage is over. They may just find the completion stage stuff boring. Or they may feel anxious about finishing, scared they can't do it. They're fine putting the clothes in the washing machine, popping the detergent in and pushing the button. But taking the clothes out and folding them is not on their agenda.

The person who fires the starting gun doesn't want to run the race.

More finishing

If we're more of a finisher, it's completing that gives us the hit. We love tidying up loose ends. We love putting on the final touches. We appreciate knowing that we've 'got the set'. Whether it's typing the last of a million addresses into a database, completing a college course or getting the kids brought up and married off, 'done and dusted' is our motto.

A strong starter may be towards (page 17), optimistic (page 43), big-picture (page 71); options (page 112),

However, don't get the impression that finishing skills are only relevant at the end of a project. Finishers can move in very quickly after the start – and take joy in doing 90 per cent of the work. What marks out finishers is that they tend to feel confused or nervous at the initial stages; they prefer to get involved once everything is up and running and it's obvious what to do next.

A bit of both

Most people actually combine starting and finishing – they can begin, they can continue, they can bring things to an end. But everyone has a bias, a comfort zone where they feel happier and more effective. So they'll shimmer with energy when things are getting going, but find the final stages of a project less inspiring. Or they'll sit quietly when the key decisions are being made but come to life when asked to put things into practice.

A strong finisher may be detail (page 71), procedures (page 112), judging (page 128).

And many people vary their bias according to context. So one of my colleagues is a true starter when it comes to leisure time hobbies: she's begun and left undone a course on tap dancing, the script she wrote in evening class and the design makeover she started to do on her back bedroom. When it comes to relationships, though, she's a rottweiler about finishing – she insists on tidying up loose ends even on tiny misunderstandings.

I, on the other hand, am more laid back about relationships. But that Art A level I started and didn't finish 34 years ago ... it still bugs me.

The starting/finishing trap

I'm friends with a famous writer who's always been superb at the first stages of any project. She erupts with enthusiasm, scrabbling to get started.

But this ability to start used to be a double-edged sword. Because she'd go dashing into huge projects – but once she'd agreed the deal, the lights went out. She struggled to trawl her way through, dragging herself kicking and screaming to the finish line.

Then, one day I met her for lunch and she looked ten years younger. Simply, she'd found a magic way round her hatred of finishing.

Now she just refuses to do big projects (like books) that would give her only one 'new start' every few years. What she takes on are short projects (like articles) that give her several new starts every week. Sure, she still grits her teeth when completing – but motivates herself by the thought of starting something new first thing tomorrow morning.

What my friend does works for her – and will work for you if you can reorganize your working life to fit. The following tips will help.

Four suggestions for starters who can't finish
- Clearly imagine what it'll feel like to finish well – and get people around you to remind you of when you've done just that.
- Learn and practise the skill of breaking down each job into small, easily doable, bite-sized chunks so you don't get frightened of them.

- Get yourself lots of help from finishers when you get into the later stages of a project – it's fine to use their completion skills to get things done.
- Remind yourself constantly that as a starter, you are irreplaceable – without you, nothing in the world would ever happen.

Me, I'm the opposite of my friend. I shudder at the very thought of starting a book, an article, a report. Even beginning an email is a wobble-opportunity for me. Starting is scary because I feel the first words I write have to be absolutely perfect – if they're not, I'm a failure. (This, by the way, is what's commonly referred to as 'writers' block'.)

My way round it is to kid myself that I don't actually start a project. At all. Ever. Instead, I see the first idea as the starting point – and as that comes from the client who sets the brief, the initial scary bit is already done by the time it gets to me. I'm just finishing off – by researching, making notes, writing, editing, proofing. I see my work as an exercise in completion and that feels much easier. I'm tempted not to call myself a writer. I'm a word tidier.

What I do works for me – and will work for you if you can start to see what you do in the right way. Here are five more tips.

Five suggestions for finishers who can't start
- Develop and practise the skill of brainstorming without feeling your thoughts need to be 'right first time' so you stop being frightened of having initial ideas.
- Get lots of support from starter people to initiate any project – it's fine to use their ideas to get things going.
- If you get paralysed with nerves, do something, anything; once you're further on in the process and feeling more confident, you can then go back and sort any mistakes you've made.
- Organize your work so you never feel as if you're starting – do

rough versions, rework several times, tell yourself that you're just tying up loose ends.
- Remind yourself constantly that as a finisher, you are irreplaceable – without you, nothing in the world would ever get completed.

Here, too, is a final tip for both starters and finishers. Learn to delegate, to ask for help, to spread the work around. Because starters need to delegate to have any hope of completing. And finishers need to delegate to have any hope of doing their own projects – rather than constantly tidying up loose ends for other people.

Three tips for anyone who needs to learn to delegate
- Give people a good reason to do what you're asking them to do – get them excited about it (this report could double our turnover, getting the shopping now will mean we can party this evening ...).
- Work out the steps that need to be taken in order to complete the task (first you need to do the research, then let's make a list of what we need to get from the shops ...).
- Be sure to reward the other person by whatever means you have available (well done, let's go down the pub, come here and have a cuddle ...).

At work

By definition, most projects have a short starting stage and a long finishing stage. That bit's pretty obvious.

But what that means is that most jobs on offer need you to do only a small amount of starting but a lot of finishing. It also means that, in all honesty, there's room in the world for only a few genuine starters – who then end up generating lots of work for finishers.

What this means is that, if you have a bias towards finishing in your personality, you're capable of many jobs. Whatever career path you follow, someone who can finish – on time, to budget and within specifications – is worth their weight in gold. Add in even a small dash of starting, so you can get things up and running as well as make them happen and you're laughing. You can enter almost any career and make a success of it.

If you're off-the-scale on finishing, uncomfortable with any sort of starting at all, then get yourself a good strong starter boss and let them set you off on every project with a clear brief. You'll reap the rewards – and the only thing you need to watch out for is being so successful that you get offered a role that demands you start things all on your own. Be wise. Say no.

And if you're off-the-scale on starting and feel sick at the very thought of finishing, be prepared for problems. Because, to be blunt, you'll get a reputation for not getting things done. And particularly at the beginning of your career, when you're not sufficiently up in the hierarchy to be valued for your initiative and vision, this will tell against you.

So do all you can to develop some finisher strategies to help you survive. Then hang in there career-wise until you're promoted to the point where you can get a team of finishers to carry out your every whim!

Oiling the wheels

So you're dealing with someone who's more of a starter. The thing that will enthrall you about them is that first-stage excitement. The thing that may irritate you is the second-stage lethargy. Because when starters get over their initial rush of adrenalin, they can simply fade away.

If you do get irritated at that fade, it may help to understand

what makes people tick?

what starters are feeling. At the very start, it feels good to be setting off on a new project. But once things are underway, they start getting in touch with all the ways that things could go wrong. They realize that they could fail at that point – so it's easier to drop it, go off and start something else. That way they avoid the pain.

Starter: 'At the beginning, I get lots of bright pictures. But once we're underway I get scared of failure and then everything seems dark and gloomy.'

So give heavy-duty starters lots of space to do their own thing at the beginning. Listen to them enthuse, encourage them to brain-storm, tell them their ideas and visions are great – because they will be.

But at the later stages, be patient. Starters are the ones who start stripping that wooden table in a flurry of enthusiasm, then lose interest and want to start stripping the wooden chair. They're the ones who have a fiery burst of energy with a new client, but then fail to follow up for repeat business. Don't get cross. Just put in the extra resources – be that a few more hands, a bit of overtime or regular hugs – to make sure the table gets completely stripped, or that the client is regularly phoned.

starting/finishing strategy

When dealing with finishers, reverse all the above. They're most scared of the starting bits – so they typically hold back and are nervous. They're all too aware that the foundations of a project are essential to its success and they worry about making mistakes. So to begin with, hold their hands, give them lots of support to get going.

Finisher: 'At the start, we need to make big decisions and they all seem important – so I get scared. Once we're underway, it all seems so much easier.'

But once things are up and running, you can leave finishers to work on – whether that's doing the mailout or doing the shopping, they'll coast through happily to the end-point. You do, however, need to remember to let them pause at that end, because completion is the place they get their buzz. And if anything has to be left on hold halfway through, then expect wobbles – leaving things half done can be physically painful; finishers need closure.

There's an extra point to bear in mind when dealing with finishers. Starters get things going and that's very impressive. So while finishers are just as valid, they often don't get the praise, the kudos from outside – plus they can feel they're being left to 'do the real work' while the starters are off doing a new project. So reward finishers, regularly and genuinely. If they're your employee, give praise and a good wage. If they're your partner, give love and cuddles.

An added hint: when visiting any workplace, it's always good to thank the receptionist, the secretary and the lady who made the tea. These finisher people are essential to the running of the company – but it might have been decades since anyone credited them for their effort!

what makes people tick?

PS: Storytelling tip 2

When giving a speech or making a business presentation, the beginning of your story will grab the starters. And by the time you're a few sentences in, the finishers will be on board. After that though, while the finishers happily hang in there, the starters may mentally drift away.

Avoid this by launching in with just the first few tantalizing details of a good anecdote to get them hooked. Keep referring back to it throughout, to keep them hooked. But don't actually finish the thing off until the very end.

Open road or step by step: options/procedures strategy

12 How do we tackle a task? Cooking a meal, running a business meeting, weeding the garden, throwing a party ... when we do something, how do we go about it? What's our strategy?

Do we tend to seek lots of alternatives, constantly find new and better ways than before? Or do we tend to rely on a system that's already in place, that's been tried and tested? In other words, are we more likely to go for lots of different options or to follow a set procedure?

Options-oriented thinking

If we're more options-driven, then we love to reinvent the wheel. Ask us for suggestions and we have several hundred at our finger-tips – plus we immediately brainstorm a long list of further possibilities. Give us any kind of project and we go for innovation, for development, for the novel and creative solution.

Want to know your own strategy? See page 273.

But ask us to use the manual or follow the system and we start grizzling and throwing a tantrum – because we just know there's a better way. (And if someone attempts to show us their better way, we immediately start thinking of ways to improve on it.)

The funniest example of options-oriented thinking I ever met was one weekend when we stayed overnight at a hotel in the North of England. When we arrived, the landlord was fascinated to hear which route we'd taken from home – and got totally hooked in to all the possible ways we could have come.

what makes people tick?

By the time we'd been shown our rooms we'd heard three options. Over dinner that night he thought up another two. And the following morning, planning how to drive back, the map came out and another few possibilities were offered. (Just to be on the safe side, in case we ever came that way again, he rang me at home two days later to make a final suggestion.)

Procedures-oriented thinking

If we're procedures-driven, then we believe that there's one right way and all that's needed is to find out what it is and run it. We want a methodology, something specified, clear and certain. In our view, the wheel doesn't need reinventing – all anyone needs to do is to use the one right wheel, in the one right way, for ever. We're great at keeping to the rules, maintaining systems, filing everything in date order and stacking our knickers by colour and size.

While options-oriented thinkers can waste time and energy in dreaming up possibilities, procedures-oriented people can waste time and energy trying to procedurize inappropriately. The moment I realized that one of my friends was a truly off-the-scale procedures person was when a drama blew up at work. This was a one-off where a takeover, plus a sudden fall in the market, plus a drama at the factory all happened in the same week.

I expected my friend to talk about the flexible ways she'd found to deal with the problem. Instead her concern was what procedures – and she actually used that word – were in place to cope with the crisis. I tried to explain to her that this level of chaos had never happened before, so there was no one perfect way to cope. It went right against the grain. 'No procedures?' she said in a tone of pure outrage. 'Well, there just should be!'

The difference

To sum up the difference between options and procedures, a real life example. When the publishers of this book were trying to decide on a title, we thought of a number of alternatives. The two most likely were these.

What Makes People Tick?, which is an options-driven title – open-ended, non-specific, with a whole range of possibilities that an options-oriented reader can imagine is included in the book.

Or *The Ultimate Guide to Personality Types*, which is a procedures-driven title, highlighting the book's systematic listing of the different kinds of personality and how they can best be used.

So we needed to decide. Should we go for the options title and alienate the procedures people? Or go for the procedures title and alienate the options people?

Luckily, a book can have a title and a subtitle. So we were able to have our cake and eat it.

Getting the best from ...

Get an options person and a procedures person together and –
guess what? As with every personality pattern, when two extremes
meet, there is misunderstanding, irritation, clashes. So whether at
home or at work, how can you get the best from the situation?

When someone is more options-driven
- Do bring them on board to revitalize or rethink – they'll love to shake things up.
- Don't bring them on board in the middle of something – they'll get frustrated at not being allowed to rethink from scratch.
- Do ask them to brainstorm, have ideas, develop new possibilities in work or life.
- Don't ask them to do something a particular way – they'll rebel or get bored.
- Do realize they see ideas as easy – so they'll be fine if you reject a first suggestion and ask for more.
- Don't expect them to commit to their first idea – they'll sulk over wasted opportunities.
- Do let them bend the rules a little – they'll love the feeling of being a rebel.
- Don't make them follow step-by-step schedules – they'll feel trapped.
- Do talk to them using phrases like – 'opportunity', 'choice', 'possibility', 'alternative', 'better way'.
- Don't get irritated because they're options-oriented – their ideas can change the world.

When someone is more procedures-driven
- Do get them defining the right way to do something – they'll specify and improve.

- Don't ask them to explore lots of possibilities – they'll feel it's a waste of time.
- Do explain a clear sequence of steps in a job – they'll remember and follow it to the letter.
- Don't offer open-ended schedules – they need to know how long each stage will – and should – take.
- Do tell them something has worked in the past – they'll then have confidence it will work in future.
- Don't expect them to do things that buck the system – they'll feel far too insecure and anxious.
- Do let them explain to you how they do things – it will clarify things in their mind.
- Don't expect them to stop proceduralizing – until you tell them 'enough' and move them on.
- Do talk to them using phrases like – 'the best way is', 'I've found this works', 'what next?'
- Don't get irritated because they're procedures-oriented – their systematic approach can change the world.

Careers advice

$ Options-oriented jobs are easy to spot. They're the ones labelled 'research and development', 'creative', 'forward thinking'. Or they don't have any of these labels, but demand enormous flexibility – teaching, for example, where you're constantly thinking up new ways to interest young minds and keep young bodies behind their desks rather than heading for the door!

So if you know you're more options-oriented, then choose the kind of career that gives you the flexibility you need and plays to your strength in rethinking things time after time.

Good jobs for options-driven people: entrepreneur, actor, management consultant, fundraiser, PR assistant, researcher, journalist, interior designer.

Predominantly procedures-oriented jobs, on the other hand, are the ones where you need to follow routines, develop systems and then run those systems in the same way, day after day after day. In these jobs, you can't suddenly decide to switch things round for a bit of variety – if you do, nasty things will happen. You can't be an electrician and suddenly decide to rewire a house a new way round for fun.

So if you know you're more procedures-oriented, choose the kind of job that will give you the stability you need and plays to your strength in running systems reliably time after time.

Good careers for procedures-driven people: bank clerk, dentist, flight attendant, beautician, paramedic, construction worker, administrator, mechanic.

However, there is a problem. Even if you have a bias towards options or procedures, you'll need to have a spread across the spectrum. Because no post will ever be completely one or the other. Every job needs a bit of development, a few new ideas throwing in, just as every job has some elements which need to be done 'the right way' or 'the way it's been done before'.

Another problem is that jobs that seem options-oriented may, nevertheless, involve hidden procedures – and that can mean that you take a job and then hate it. I was once given a manicure by an options-driven trainee beautician. And from her comments, it was obvious she thought she was getting into an options-oriented profession – after all, beauty work involves dealing with different clients every day, doesn't it? The problem is, beauty work is actually very procedures-driven; you have to massage, wax and give facials in roughly the same way, time after time after time. No surprise then that at my next appointment, I was told that the trainee had 'got bored and left'.

There is an even bigger problem: whole career areas can actually shift from one extreme to the other as years go by. The typical shift is from options to procedures, as staff develop systems and then stick to them, or when business practice in a firm gets formalized and more set in stone.

Take the following example. As mentioned before, good teachers have to have a large pinch of options-orientation. But the recent bureaucratization of education in Britain has involved teachers needing to fill in many more forms and follow many more procedures than they're used to.

Which is one reason why, over the past decade or so, there has been a mass exodus from the British education system – of staff who have found themselves to be options-driven pegs in procedures-motivated holes!

Love is ... options

♥ At work, options and procedures can both hack it. In relationships, the options approach always wins.

You can proceduralize an office system, but you can't proceduralize a friendship, a courtship, a marriage.

An options person may be in-time (page 62), big-picture (page 71), difference (page 80), starting (page 103), perceiving (page 128).

The problem is that if you have a more procedures-oriented personality, it can be very tempting to think you can do just that – that you can find the underlying 'perfect way' to run your relationship. You believe that if you fulfil precisely what your partner wants, they'll be happy: that if you bring your husband a cup of tea in bed every morning for a quarter of a century, he will therefore stay and keep on loving you; that in bed, two minutes doing this and four minutes doing that will result in an automatic orgasm (don't laugh – it's been known).

what makes people tick?

This kind of procedures thinking is what drives the current fascination with incredibly prescriptive relationships books such as *The Rules*, which gave a whole generation of procedures women the totally false security of thinking that if they followed steps A to Z, they'd land the husband of their choice.

But in fact, when it comes to love, there are no rules and there are no procedures. There are guidelines that work for most of humanity. But you, your partner and your relationship are unique.

So the bottom line is this.

If what you're doing in your relationship works, then carry on doing it. Every relationship has its procedures, its rituals which are familiar and comfortable and which bring a sense of security – and love – to you both.

A procedures person may be through-time (page 62), detail (page 71), sameness (page 80), finishing (page 103), judging (page 128).

But if what you're doing in your relationship begins to stop working, then whatever kind of personality you have, options or procedures, you will need to start behaving like an options-driven person. Which means do something different – anything, to change the dynamic and breathe fresh air into what is happening.

And if that doesn't work, do something different again. And again. And again. A recent survey by British marriage charity One Plus One showed that the single most important factor that determines whether couples survive is flexibility.

So if you want to keep your relationship stable, fresh and working, remember those three little words. Options, options, options.

PS: Avoiding group chaos

 If you're directing a group, whether it's friends, colleagues or kids, giving them lots of options won't work. The options-oriented folk will mentally start looking out for other possibilities and so get distracted from what you're saying. Meanwhile, the procedures-driven people will just get confused and paralysed. And everyone will head off in a different direction, leaving you trying to cope with chaos.

Instead, give clear directions with one step completed before you present the next. Yes, the options-driven participants may feel a bit trapped. But that's preferable to the disaster scenario of trying to run a group without any procedures at all!

what makes people tick?

Jump or be pushed: proactivity/reactivity strategy

13 So there's a job to be done – doesn't matter what. A big project at work – or just opening the post. A big house move afoot – or just clearing the loft. How do we tackle it? Do we jump? Or get pushed? Rush in and get going on things or hang back and wait for other people? Most of us combine a bit of both – with a slight bias to one or the other.

More proactive

If we're more proactive, we're more likely to initiate action. We tend to look around, see what's to be done, decide we'll do it and make a move.

We'll be the one first up to lead the standing ovation. We'll ring room service at 2am in the morning. We'll zoom straight to the information desk when the flight's been delayed.

We take things on board as our responsibility, we accept the risks, we get going. Our mottos are 'he who hesitates is lost', 'nothing ventured nothing gained', plus our new one, the line from the Nike ad, 'just do it'.

Want to know your own strategy? See page 275.

All this doesn't mean that proactive people are necessarily big on confidence. It does mean that the 'do it' motivation kicks in early and without the need for permission from others.

My friend Jacinta is the most proactive person I know. She says that, like most of us, she often has stage fright when treading the boards of life. But that didn't stop her applying for a post in the European Parliament straight from university, going on a meditation course up a Tibetan mountain, moving to America for a top job – and taking several foreign trips a year, every year, on her own.

When the Los Angeles earthquake hit, Jacinta was in her car and up there volunteering before anyone else had dusted themselves down. Other people think about it. Jacinta does it.

Starters get off on the first stages of a project – but may not be eager to act. Proactives get going – at whatever stage of the project they are.

More reactive

If we're reactive, we'll hang back. We're not scared of hard work – once others make a move, then we're in there grafting. And we're not incapable – we can do things, of course we can. But we'll never be first over the top.

Reactives can tend to have an unfairly bad press – the world celebrates self-starters. But being reactive doesn't mean that we lack confidence or energy. It does mean we like to be sure that something is ours to do, that we're not butting in, that we've been invited. It does mean we check that the job is relevant, appropriate and doable before we start.

It also means that we assess the risks before accepting an invitation. A proactive will agree with creative writing guru Julie Cameron that if you 'leap … the net will appear'. A reactive likes to set up the net, check the ropes then spend several days revising their leaping techniques. (And in fact, because of that, they're far less likely to fall.)

Reactivity has a downside, however, when we have nothing to 'react' to. If clients aren't beating a path to the door, a true reactive will not go out on the streets looking for them. If friends aren't ringing with party invites, a true reactive will not pick up the phone.

And, in all honesty, when it comes to building a social life – or a career – that can be a problem.

what makes people tick?

Learning to jump

There are pros and cons about being proactive or reactive. Extremely proactive people – apologies to you if you are one – can be seen as bossy, meddling, tactless.

But on balance, high reactivity is the greater of two evils because it leaves you out of control. If you wait for that invitation to act – for your lover to ring, for your boss to give you that promotion – you might just wait forever. The most off-the-scale reactive I know did wait forever rather than make a play for the girl of his dreams. He confided in me weekly about how he wanted her, but felt the time wasn't right, the mood wasn't right and she wasn't ready. When she announced her engagement to someone else, he was gutted – but explained that now she'd made her choice, it wasn't up to him to put a spanner in the works by declaring his love. That was 30 years ago. He still mourns her. It's a true – and terrifying – story.

Of course you'd never be that silly (would you?). But just in case, here are some simple ways to become more proactive than you already are. Think of a goal, any goal, big or small – getting a new flat, getting a job, getting laid, getting the cupboard cleared, getting the filing done ...

1 The first thing that stops people being proactive is thinking that they're not the person who should be taking action. So, think it through. Will anyone else initiate things if you don't? Chances are, the onus is on you.

2 The next thing that stops people being proactive is feeling they haven't been invited to act. So, consider, are you sure other people aren't waiting for you to show interest, to make the first move?

3 The next thing that stops people being proactive is feeling the timing is wrong. So, ask yourself: if not now, when? To paraphrase the Roman motto, if you don't 'seize the day' then it will very soon be sunset.

4 The next thing that stops people being proactive is feeling that taking action is too big and risky a leap. So, work out the tiniest, least risky next step you need to take towards your goal.

5 The next thing that stops people being proactive is not knowing exactly how to act. So, once you know your first tiny 'step', imagine clearly how you might take it. Find someone who's already done what you're planning to do and ask them to coach you in how to succeed.

6 The next thing that stops people being proactive is not knowing how to overcome blocks. So, imagine what problems might arise when you take that tiny step – lack of skills, lack of knowledge, lack of support from others? List the problems. Then find a solution to each of them.

7 The next thing that stops people being proactive is thinking they have to sort every last detail before they get going. But it's

what makes people tick?

usually fine to go ahead before everything's done and dusted. So, take the 'next step' whether or not you feel ready. You can go back and redo it if things go wrong.

8 If the step you take works and you move closer to your goal, what then? Then simply go back to number 4, identify the next step you need to take, and continue on through the sequence as before.

Career tracks, career sidings

For most jobs you need to be proactive and reactive. There aren't many projects, let alone entire career tracks, where you do everything on your own initiative, just as there aren't many posts where someone tells you exactly what to do on a second-by-second basis.

But if you're more proactive than reactive, then you'll be happier with more action and more individual responsibility – anything where you can pick up the ball and run with it. Just beware of two things.

Good careers for proactives: sales, holiday rep, supervisor, entrepreneur, journalist, fundraiser, police.

First, beware of the flak that will fly when you're overly proactive without management permission. A highly proactive friend of mine, in her first week working for a small charity, was asked to start researching national companies who could eventually be approached for donations. But before her line-manager had had her morning coffee, my friend was on the phone actually asking for the money – nooooo, far too early in the process!

Second, beware of applying for jobs that seem proactive, but are actually reactive. Employers have got seduced by the term 'proactivity', so lots of firms think that they want someone way off on the proactive extreme when in fact what they want is someone who's balanced between the two ends of the spectrum – or even someone who's actually quite reactive.

I spotted a situations vacant ad in our local paper last week, written as if to drag the proactives in off the street. 'If you're tired of the waiting game' it read 'call us now and get moving ...' Only problem was, I happen to know that the job being offered was a classic reactive post – an assistant who isn't expected to even blink unless their boss gives them permission. So I do wonder who'll be appointed. And how long they'll last.

Good careers for reactives: call centre employee, waiter, retail assistant, customer service worker, receptionist.

If you're more reactive than proactive then you'll do very well in 'executive' jobs where someone else has the idea and you do the executing. Secretary, project assistant, anything with a tight management structure will suit.

Watch, though, that you don't end up in a career siding. A very talented, but very reactive, friend of mine stayed in a dead-end job for six years, waiting for something better to come along. She got to the point where she hoped her boss would sack her, so she could leave. But still she didn't budge.

She might still be there today – frustrated, unhappy and reactively stuck – had not a much less experienced (but far more proactive) colleague decided to set up his own company. He invited my friend to join him and – responding to the request with her usual enthusiastic reactivity – she did. Given that nudge, she was fine, able to respond to the invitation and accept the risks.

It's working well for both of them. She provides the expertise. He provides the initiative. They'll be fine.

PS: Turning a reactive proactive

Say someone in your life drives you wild because they're so reactive. They definitely won't shift character just because you *want* them to. But, given that they're so reactive, they might shift character if you *tell* them to.

Try this. Define clearly when, where, how and what you want them to do. Then motivate them strongly by explaining – and if possible, demonstrating – just how delighted you'll be when they do it. You may well mysteriously find them doing more in future – and all you have to do then is forget that they're acting on your orders!

Mover-shaker or flow: judging/perceiving strategy

14 Do we adapt to life? Or do we expect life to adapt to us? When it comes to action, do we let things happen to us or make things happen round us?

Want to know your own strategy? See page 276.

This personality pattern means that some people need to organize the world to their needs, their targets, their desires. Others let the world run on – they just love to be in the flow, never worrying if they're not on top of what's happening.

More judging

Judgers and influencers are different. A judger organizes their life; an influencer wants power over people.

If we're more of a judger, we seriously like to make our mark on the things around us. We observe what's happening with an eagle eye, to see if it fits our plan. If it does, we check it off. If it doesn't, we act to order it, tidy it, settle it and sort it.

We rarely wait – we move in immediately we can to make decisions, organize, get closure. We wriggle if asked to chill out – we like to be on top of things the whole time. For us, the song is 'I'll tell you what I want, what I really really want ...', courtesy of The Spice Girls.

More perceiving

If we're more of a perceiver, we love to let life flow past us. So we watch what's happening, note it, accept it – and then let it go. We're actually not too worried about making the world match our expectations or making things bend to us – we're happy to bend to them.

 what makes people tick?

We wait to make decisions, are happy if decisions are made for us, react spontaneously and keep our options open. We forget evaluations, lists and plans and schedules – even, forget worrying about worrying. Our favourite song is perhaps 'Let it be' by The Beatles.

What's the difference?

An off-the-scale judger at work grabs her career by the scruff of the neck and makes it happen, promotion by careful promotion. Meanwhile, a perceiver has an 'interesting' CV, because she always takes what comes along, job by job. And an off-the-scale judger worries from day one about whether her relationship is the real thing, whilst a perceiver relaxes into love, but is equally accepting when it starts to fade.

Be prepared for surprises, though. As with so many patterns, judging and perceiving are often contextual. So a judger at home, who irons the teatowels every Monday without fail, may be a perceiver at work, with an open door policy and a laissez-faire attitude to the sales targets. And a judger at work, who likes to be totally on top of the schedules, can let it all hang out when they're with their kids at the weekend.

How not to murder your spouse

Get a judger living with a perceiver and the fur will fly.

Because we're not talking a surface personality pattern here – we're talking fundamental approach to life. And if one of you is a judger and the other is a perceiver, then your life approaches are truly going to be chalk and cheese.

More, they'll be chalk and cheese that argue a lot. Because a judger's need for order can make a perceiver feel pinned and

Perceiver.   Judger.

restless, while a perceiver's flow-with-the-river philosophy can make a judger feel amazingly insecure. Let me give you a trivial example, but one that had my husband and I at each other's throats for months until we realized what was happening.

I'm a judger; so each morning, as I wake, I like to think about my day, sort out what I'm going to do, get it planned. Even at weekends, that little mental routine is my wake-up call that energizes and gets me going. So I saw nothing wrong, when my husband and I were first living together, in waking on a Saturday morning, snuggling up to him and then asking in a sleepy voice 'what have you got planned for today, sweetie?'.

What I didn't know was that to my perceiver husband this was the ultimate button pusher. Lying there holding me in his arms, he was experiencing something akin to being hit repeatedly on the head with a mallet. He was thinking 'Nooooo! Don't ask me what I've got planned. I don't want to think about that. I just want to do things as they come up. Don't make me.' We wondered for ages why weekend mornings were not our best time.

what makes people tick?

A judger often has the more controlled attitude to time typical of a through-time person.

Then we found out about perceivers and judgers, and realized what we were doing wrong. Now my husband understands that I need at least a little structure to my Saturdays, so he lets me know on Friday evening roughly what he's got in store over the weekend. I, on the other hand, realize that he doesn't want to be pinned down to an organized action plan on his days off, so I don't ask that question – particularly when we're snuggled up.

A perceiver often has the more flexible attitude to time typical of an in-time person.

That's a small instance – but the judger/perceiver difference can ripple through your whole life. A perceiver may hoard, where a judger will clear out the drawers every three months and file what's left in date order. A perceiver may be happy with 'last minute' holidays, where a judger will wobble if the itinerary isn't fixed 12 months in advance.

How do you cope? The answer, as with so many personality patterns, is twofold – acceptance and balance.

You need to accept your partner's different personality patterns, realizing that though your way may feel comfortable, theirs is just as valid. There's nothing wrong with letting the world go by – just as there's nothing wrong with getting it organized. So don't simply pin perceivers down – keep options open, keep things spontaneous. And don't trash judgers' need for commitment – focus on organization and structure, let them feel things are totally sorted.

It will help if you realize that the two subpatterns, judging and perceiving, work superbly well together. So perceivers can help judgers to chill out, be flexible. Judgers can help perceivers to be more organized, more effective. Living together can become an easy and elegant dance, where one of you supplies the day-to-day planning and the other adds a philosophy of 'don't worry, be happy'.

Break your boundaries

 Want to develop your range? Particularly with judging/perceiving, the best way is to do things you wouldn't normally do.

And yes, that may make you feel uncomfortable. If you're a judger, the thought of becoming more laid back may send you into a flurry of concern – what if I don't get things done, what if it all goes pear-shaped? If you're a perceiver, the thought of becoming more organized may send a chill of fear up your spine – what if I turn anally retentive, what if I lose my *joie de vivre?*

But if you can hang on in through the discomfort, you'll learn that stepping outside your natural personality doesn't mean the end of the world. So relax, give it a go, and the 'against the grain' behaviour will slowly bed in. You won't lose your essential self. Instead, you'll find yourself with a wider – and more useful – repertoire.

Four developmental tasks for people who judge more than perceive
- Do something spontaneous – not planning it meticulously, but simply doing it now.
- Allow a bit of chaos into your life – leave the washing up until tomorrow or leave your clothes on the floor when you go to bed.
- Choose one decision you 'have to' make today and postpone making it until next weekend.
- Treat yourself to something totally self-indulgent and laid back. Like a cream cake. Or a trashy novel. Or a long lie in.

what makes people tick?

Four developmental tasks for people who perceive more than judge

- Note three things you're going to do today. Then do them. No excuses.
- Plan your day – morning, afternoon, evening. Then stick to the plan.
- Tidy up one room in your house. Or if that feels too hard, one drawer.
- Find something that bugs you or bugs someone in your life – the bulb that needs replacing, the plant that needs repotting, the make-up that's slightly the wrong shade. Then sort it.

PS: As you age

The passing of time doesn't just bring on the wrinkles. It also shifts your judging and perceiving patterns.

So adolescents can be serious perceivers – not because they don't want to be organized, but because they feel over-organized by the outside world. They need to redress the balance by being easy on themselves and 'letting it all hang out'.

But as people become more adult, confident, socially powerful, they may give judging a try, getting more on top of life, quite simply organizing it to a higher degree. Come the arrival of children – who make life feel totally disorganized – and any judging tendency shoots to the max, just to keep on top of things.

As you get older, responsibilities fall away. You can tend to get more philosophical, more laid back and slide slowly into being a 'let the world go by' perceiver.

HOW PERSONALITY WORKS 4

Get in a relationship with someone and your whole personality can shift. Not just with lovers. Make a friend, meet a colleague, even have a baby – put two human beings together and their personalities will start to spark.

One person behaves one way, the other reacts to that, the first person reacts back. You've no choice but to affect each other. For example ...

- **You may grow more like each other. Put a pessimist in an office team and within weeks you'll all be groaning. Add a new, optimistic flatmate to an existing menage and the rest of you perk up in response.**
- **You may grow just slightly apart, to cover all the bases and balance each other out. You both start off as sensation-seekers – but one of you has to settle down a bit otherwise you'd both kill yourselves. You both start off as sameness-oriented people – but one of you has to go for novelty otherwise you'd both end up in a rut.**
- **You may grow into the role you always grow into, whoever you're with, filling the same position in a relationship, even with different partners. Pair with a starter and you do the finishing. But pair with a finisher and mysteriously they turn into a starter and you do finishing once again.**

Personality isn't rigid. It bends and shapes according to whom you're with.

Higher state of consciousness: awareness of others scale

15 Every day of our lives, we meet other people. But how aware are we of what's going on for them? How neatly can we step into their shoes? Do we notice what their words and body language are really communicating – or are we more aware of what's going on for us?

More aware

If we naturally pay attention to what's going on for other people, then we're usually able to pick up all the cues people send. Crucially, that's not just words but body language too. We notice these nonverbal signals, feel them inside, step into the other person's world, see through their eyes. We end up truly, deeply (sometimes madly) understanding others' experience.

Want to know where you fall on this scale? See page 278.

So we'll spot when our partner is tired, when a dinner guest needs more wine, when the colleague across the boardroom table is at boiling point. We'll identify with that scared child, angry lover, shocked colleague. Our response is often frighteningly accurate, our insights seriously useful.

The retail assistant who realizes without asking when a customer wants to be left alone to browse will have a high level of awareness. As will the nurse or counsellor who senses the nerves of a patient and – without even thinking about it – knows exactly what to say to calm them down.

Less aware

At totally the other end of the extreme, there's the person who is hardly aware of others' experience at all, who concentrates primarily on their own thoughts and feelings. They're the one who needs flashcards to realize when someone fancies them, who takes things just too far in an argument, who wraps up a meeting too soon, lets it go on too long or makes that crucial decision without realizing that there's any opposition.

Why the difference?

But why on earth would any of us be less aware of others – what could stop us paying attention to outside experience? There are two main factors.

Awareness is based on taking in all the cues people give out – verbal and nonverbal. So a lack of awareness may simply be down to not noticing the subtler, nonverbal cues. The least aware person I know is an incredibly short-sighted writer who literally doesn't see what people do and so relies on what they say. She doesn't actually register the grimace, the smile or the slumped posture that would tell her what someone's feeling – so she concentrates on her own experience and only gets a fraction of the whole story.

Alternatively, it can be that we notice all the signals, verbal and nonverbal, but don't interpret them correctly – maybe because we've never been taught to do so. Some children grow up in families where empathy is at a premium – or where they're actively discouraged from awareness because it's seen as weak. Boys, for example, are much more likely to be told to get in there, fists flailing, than to try to understand what's going on for others.

When someone's locked inside their head

Get together with someone who is unaware of others and you'll quickly find yourself feeling odd. We're talking a minority of people here – one in fourteen. But when you meet them, it's a very strange experience.

Because someone who's not aware is largely only listening to your words – and taking little account at all of the 97 per cent of your communication that's nonverbal. So they're actually missing the majority of what's going on. And if they're missing it, then by definition they're not responding to it. Within minutes, you can feel that they're ignoring you, misinterpreting you, wilfully overriding you. They're not, of course. But it will still feel odd.

I remember attending a course given by a well respected history lecturer who was amazingly unaware of others. When on the

Highly aware.

 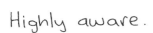

podium, reading his prepared speech and not having to interact with the audience, he was fine.

But in the meal breaks, you really didn't want to sit at his table because he never noticed that the dirty jokes he was telling were completely unacceptable. I spotted the problem – so I wasn't surprised to overhear the course organizer say to him quietly that what he was doing wasn't appropriate.

The result was instant mortification and apology. From then on, this brilliant man was still unaware of others – so tended to talk on and over everybody. But, once he knew there was a problem, the dirty jokes came to an abrupt halt.

So how can you check whether a person is doing uncomfortable things from nastiness or lack of awareness? Simple. Give them a clear nonverbal signal and see if they notice and react. Let your gaze shoot away – do they turn to see what you're looking at? Drop a pencil – do they half bend to help you pick it up? Cough – do they pause in talking? If none of these get through to them, you're dealing with someone who's largely unaware.

But then what do you do? How do you sort things so a person understands what you mean, starts reacting to your communications.

It's actually quite easy – all you need to do is stop being subtle and spell it out. Because this person is relying heavily on words for their information, all you need to do is put into words what you mean and they'll be far more responsive. So tell them, 'I'm feeling upset,' or say, 'I think you've misunderstood me.'

This may seem far too crass – you'd hate it if someone spelled things out to you like that, so you expect everyone else to hate it too. But remember that the person who's unaware needs your words to alert them to problems, to get them to listen to you and to stop listening quite so much to themselves. Hence you're doing them a favour if you tell them directly – if tactfully – that they're not reading you correctly.

There may, of course, be other things going on which mean that a person won't necessarily cooperate or give in. But largely, if you spell something out in words, even a less aware person will take stuff on board.

Stepping into shoes ... not on toes

Let's be brutally honest here. Having a low score on this personality pattern is a problem. Quite simply, you miss out. You miss out on what other people are telling you. You miss out on really experiencing their thoughts and feelings. And you can end up misunderstanding, misinterpreting, getting negative feedback, reducing people to tears.

So if this sounds familiar, here's what to do
- Improve your reading of body language skills, through reading books or taking courses (see page 293). With this knowledge, start paying attention to the nonverbal signals as well as the words you hear.
- Get people whose feelings matter to you – lovers, relatives, friends – to be really direct about what they feel. That will help you start to calibrate accurately what they say with what they look like.
- Don't rely on people's words – they make up only 7 per cent of communication. When reaching important conclusions or taking vital decisions, it may be useful to get the opinion of someone more people-aware – they may well have spotted clues and drawn conclusions you haven't.
- Be wary of jobs that are extremely people-based – and if you're already in such a job and hitting problems, then acknowledge that. You might be better off in a non-interactive role – something technical, knowledge-based, word-based or machine-based.

On the other hand, if you're highly aware of others' experience, life isn't necessarily a bed of roses. You can misunderstand people because you're overwhelmed by the signals they're giving out. And this can lead to 'negative mind-reading' – you sense some emotion in another person, then jump to the (incorrect) conclusion that it's aimed at you and in a negative way.

So if this sounds familiar, here's what to do

- Improve your ability to switch off from people's signals, particularly when these are affecting your ability to think clearly or act decisively. Assertiveness training will help you do this – see the Resources section on page 293.
- Make a pact with people you trust – lovers, relatives, friends – that they'll tell you if they disapprove of or are angry with you. Then, unless they actually say so, trust that they don't feel negative and allow yourself to relax around them.
- Don't rely on people's body language signals alone – they are a major part of communication, but not the conscious part. So it can be useful, particularly when you are under stress, to tune out the nonverbal signals you are receiving – so that you can clearly listen to the words people are saying.
- Steer clear of jobs which involve high levels of people interaction, particularly those that involve conflict, like customer service. The strong emotions you're bombarded with in that kind of job will make your life very uncomfortable – because you feel them more deeply than most people.

what makes people tick?

PS: Instant divorce

If you're in love, surely you should be as aware as possible of one ♥
another? Watching your partner to catch every expression, listening to catch every verbal nuance, imagining you are one another,
blending every thought and emotion ... Isn't that the way to really
become close as a couple?

Well, not necessarily. Because if you're too aware of each other's
every signal, then you can simply end up playing mood tennis –
with each of you overinterpreting what they see and hear and
hallucinating all sorts of negative reactions.

To see this at its worst, stand in any supermarket checkout
queue during rush hour late Friday, and watch endless lines of
couples – all too aware of other's reactions – trigger each other off
into a weekend of rows.

Party animal: extroversion/introversion strategy

16 Of course we know all about the personality pattern of extroversion and introversion. Don't we? Well, not necessarily. There's a lot of confusion about what this pattern really is.

Extroversion doesn't mean we're the life and soul of the party – what extroversion means is that when our batteries need recharging, we do that best in company. Introversion doesn't mean we're shy or 'sad' – what introversion means is that when our batteries need recharging, we do that best alone.

More extrovert

If people give us energy, then we're more extrovert than introvert. We get our emotional revival from others, from talking and listening, from swapping attention, encouragement and support. We love the interactive aspects of work, the phone calls, the meetings, the post-work pub crawls. We'll spend our lunch hour in the canteen, our evenings seeing friends and, when we're tired, we'll pick up the phone.

Want to know your own strategy? See page 280.

Be clear about this. We may not necessarily have many deep relationships, or get close to people. We may not even believe that people are all that central in the grand scheme of things – affiliation may not be our prime motivator (see McClelland's motivator modes, page 5). But if we are extrovert, when it comes to staying sane, what we need is people.

what makes people tick?

More introvert

If people drain our energy, then we're more introvert than extrovert. We'll relax when alone, basking in the peace of our own inner world. We'll sit quite happily watching TV or just thinking – but put us in a room with lots of other people for more than an hour or two and we start to fade. We'll spend our lunch hour walking in the park, our evenings on the Web and, when we're tired, we'll read a book.

Again, be aware: introverts aren't necessarily people haters. When we interact, we may do it eagerly and with great social competence. When we have relationships, we may have lots of very close ones. We may work well in teams. We may be dyed-in-the-wool affiliators. But when it comes to staying sane, then at the end of the day what we need is solitude.

Ambiversion

In fact, most of us need a mixture of 'people' and 'solitude'. So you could call most people 'ambiverts' – sometimes extrovert, sometimes introvert.

Plus, extroversion/introversion balance will vary according to how life is going and what state you're in. I had a friend who worked as a teacher, surrounded by students all day – and was heavily introverted in terms of craving peace and solitude. Then he moved into industry, got his own office and a lot more control over his environment. Given such daily doses of sanity time, he suddenly became far more extroverted in the evenings, a positive party animal!

I've heard friends with families report the same phenomenon in reverse. BC (before child) you crave interaction; AC, all you want is peace and quiet.

You're like this because ...

So, how do you become an extrovert or introvert? According to psychologist Hans Eysenck, it's all down to the nervous system you were born with.

Because the most stimulating thing for any human being's nervous system is another human being. So if you're born with a robust nervous system, people interaction will enervate you – you'll be an extrovert. If you're born with a sensitive nervous system, people interaction will stress you – so you'll be an introvert. (The male gender in general tends to have a more vulnerable nervous system and so men are more likely to be introvert.)

But biology isn't the only reason why you might be extrovert or introvert. Your upbringing counts too. So if you're an only child, used to long periods of solitude, you may find the very thought of people intrusive and be an off-the-scale introvert – or you may react by needing people, people, people all the time.

Extrovert letting their hair down.

Introvert letting their hair down.

what makes people tick?

Conversely, if you're brought up in a 'people first' culture, you may be desperate for time alone. Or you may find solitude draining and be an off-the-scale extrovert. I once worked with a girl who came from a family where everyone hung out together all the time. She simply wasn't used to being by herself; so much so that if she was left alone in the office for more than a few minutes, she started to wobble.

Living with a party animal ... or not

If someone is seriously extrovert or introvert at work, it won't really bite. Sure, you may find them wanting to chat while everyone wants to get their head down – or to get their head down while everyone's chatting.

But their extrovert/introvert personality won't really affect the way you work alongside them day to day – simply because during that working day, they won't get to the point of needing their batteries recharged.

If someone is seriously introvert or extrovert in your social group, you'll notice more. The introverts will want to meet you one on one or run the relationship through emails. The extroverts will dominate your dinner table and insist on hanging out with a crowd. But all you really need to do here is respect this – not throw a temper tantrum when your introvert friend mysteriously has to wash their hair every time you throw a party, not feel rejected when your extrovert friend needs all their mates present, not just you, to celebrate their birthday.

Where extroversion/introversion really hits home is if you're in a partnership. Because it's in the comfort of their own home, with their nearest and dearest, that people are usually most in need of battery recharge – and so are most likely to run heavy extrovert or introvert numbers.

And a few years into your relationship, after the first flush of love fades, the differences may well start to bite.

If you're both introvert, you may well have stopped talking to each other at all and be drifting apart – or have stopped interacting with the world and be hermits. If you're both extroverts, you may well have started to resent the fact that you both need lots of inter-action and attention – visiting friends can be hell if each of you is feeling upstaged by the other.

If there's a mix, then whichever of you is extrovert may start to feel rejected by the other's tendency to withdraw – introverts are adept at 'close down' body language signals. The most introvert boyfriend I ever had was quite happy to spend several hours in my company reading – he loved me lots, but didn't actually want to talk or touch, which, frankly, drove me crazy.

Or, whichever of you is introvert may start to feel invaded by the other's tendency to talk the whole time. There's nothing more toe-curlingly embarrassing than a serious extrovert who hasn't clocked that their voice has all the subtlety of a loud-hailer.

So if you're living with someone who's more extrovert, remember that ...

- **they need people to keep their spirits up – and that's other people as well as you**
- **to make sense of what's happening to them, they need to talk about it**
- **they need to feel trusted – so confide your thoughts, experiences, feelings**
- **they feel supported by you – so even when meeting others, they like you along**
- **if you're introvert, they're providing you with something special – contacts**
- **if you're also extrovert, relax – there's enough attention for both of you**

 what makes people tick?

If you're living with someone who's more introvert, remember that ...

- **they need internal time to stay sane - they sometimes won't want you around**
- **they don't need to talk things through - so silence doesn't mean they don't care**
- **too much interaction hurts - so a quick word is better than a long explanation**
- **they like one-on-ones - so don't get jealous if they spend time alone with friends**
- **if you're extrovert, they're providing you with something special - silence**
- **if you're also introvert, don't stop communicating - if you do, you'll stop loving!**

Introvert's survival guide

If you're a happy introvert, don't change. Sure, our culture tends to rate extroverts. But some of the world's most successful people are introverts.

But, whilst there's no reason to change your deep personality, it could be that – particularly at work – you need to *act* more like an extrovert. You know you should go down the wine bar with the team but you just can't face it. You know you're low-energy at meetings but you just feel peopled out. What can you do to act different?

How to survive the world as an introvert
- Limit your people contact. Have short lunches rather than extended ones. Send emails or texts rather than phoning. The effect on others is more or less the same; the comfort factor for you will be far higher.

- Learn to listen genuinely – and to give acknowledgment signals to show you're listening. This won't just increase your social competence; it'll be less of a strain than having to chat. Plus, listening is the secret to clinching almost any deal – and, incidentally, to seducing almost any partner.
- Hone your verbal skills. Learn to ask good questions, make good responses. Make each individual interaction rewarding for both parties and people won't notice any discomfort you may feel whilst interacting.
- In groups, don't feel you have to get in and mix the whole time. Manage it as a series of one to ones – and if you get stuck with a large number of people, simply move on and find another individual to talk to.
- Remember that internal time is not an optional extra for you, it's a necessity for your sanity. So, particularly when you're under stress, take enough time alone. You'll then find it much easier to mix when you have to.

PS: Perfect dinner parties

To plan the seating round a social table, work out first who's extrovert and who's introvert. Place extroverts opposite each other at table head or midsides, so they get access to people, eye contact, conversations. Place the introverts in between and at the corners, where they're not so exposed and can withdraw occasionally if they want. Result? A table full of happy bunnies.

Me or you? External/internal inspiration strategy

17 When deciding what to do – or say, or think, or feel – where do we take our inspiration? Whose lead do we follow? Whose wishes do we respect? This pattern outlines the possibilities.

At one end of the spectrum, there's getting inspired externally by other people – happily following what our family, workmates or partner suggest. At the other end of the spectrum, there's getting inspired internally – relying entirely on our own personal sense of what to do.

More externally-inspired

If we tend towards the external end of the spectrum, we make decisions on the guidance we receive from others. Of course we have our own ideas, but we'll be energized and motivated by outside feedback. We'll consciously take into account the people in our lives – what they think, feel, say or desire. And sponge-like, we'll pick up their values and criteria.

Remember the vultures in *Jungle Book*, checking out 'Whadda you wanna do ... nah, whadda YOU wanna do?' Externals, every one.

Of course, we don't necessarily come straight out and ask advice. We do note what others want, get motivated by it, act to fulfil it. So even if we keep quiet during a meeting, we go along with the majority vote. Even if we do switch the furniture round while our spouse is out, we'll do it in a way that exactly fits their criteria.

Want to know your own strategy? See page 282.

More internally-inspired

If we tend towards the internal end of the spectrum, we'll make decisions on what we ourselves feel is right. Sure, we read the books, ask the experts, phone a friend. We may well subscribe to a moral code, cultural norm, religious belief. And we care what people think, just as much as anyone. It's just that when the chips are down, we're the final arbiter; we check out inside ourselves what feels right and we do it.

The more internally-inspired someone is, the more individual they'll be. Like the woman who walks into the Ritz dressed in track suit and trainers, quite prepared to argue the toss with the maître d'. Or the man who goes to the opera in full black tie on Saturday evening, but spends Sunday afternoons skateboarding. Stirling Moss, the famous British Formula One Champion, rides a scooter to work – odds on he's internal!

What's the difference?

The core difference between externally and internally inspired is not that external people take notice of what others want and internal people don't.

The real difference is this. An externally-inspired person gets motivated by a conscious awareness of what people want. When they wonder what to do, they check out mentally what others would prefer – perhaps even getting an inner representation of someone being pleased. Then they think 'that will bring a smile to so-and-so's face – I'll do it.'

When an internally-inspired person wonders what to do, they also fleetingly check out mentally – but they get a strong inner sense of the way to go without any conscious sense of whether others approve or not. Then they think 'That's the right thing to do – I'll do it.'

Externally motivated.

Internally motivated.

It's not that internal people have never been influenced by others. They regularly take on board parents' morals, teachers' instructions, role models' ideals. And these values are deeply embedded – so deeply embedded that internal people typically have very little sense of where their values originate from. Yes, internals are aware of whether a decision/action feels right and they're aware of their own inner motivation – but they may not be aware of the outside influence that's created that motivation.

And if faced with a here and now demand or their own inner sense of right and wrong, it's no contest. For internally-inspired people, the inner sense wins out every time.

This (genuine) email interchange says it all, really.

- *Very external person*, influenced by the here and now thought of the boss's disapproval: 'I'm worried I'll get into trouble sending you an email in company time.'

- *Very internal person*, influenced by a lifelong belief that labour deserves reward and completely uninfluenced by the real possibility of the boss looming: 'Blow that. I think we've worked hard enough that we deserve a bit of fun.'
- *Very external person*, now influenced by their friend's comment: 'Yes, you're right. OK, let's carry on.'

Getting along with

Forty per cent of people in the world are externally-inspired. Forty per cent of the people in the world are internally-inspired. And 20 per cent mix and match. So whatever your strategy, on average half of the people you meet on a day-to-day basis are going to have a different one from yours. How do you handle that?

More externally-inspired

People who are more external need to know what you're thinking. Without that, they start to feel confused, insecure, literally shaky. With it, their inner energy kicks in.

So they get most motivated when given positive feedback, most demotivated if criticized, and utterly wobbled if faced with conflicting imperatives.

I once saw a highly external male colleague take a long loo break during a heavy business meeting. He said he had a tummy upset. Yeah, right. In my opinion, this guy's stomach had been upset – not physically, but emotionally – as two departments both demanded completely different things from him. And his externally-oriented personality sobbed 'nooooooo'.

If anyone disagrees with anything I say, I not only retract it, but also deny under oath that I ever said it. (Tom Lehrer, satirist and off-the-scale external)

So when with an external person, stay focused and positive. Tell them how pleased you are at what they're achieving and never, never give them conflicting instructions. If you yourself are internally-inspired, you may sigh 'that's so sad' – but external people need handling this way in order to stay motivated and sane.

More internally-inspired

People who are more internally-inspired can come across as incredibly self-assured. Arrogant even. The bottom line is that they feel uncomfortable when asked to take into account the outside world. They've got their principles. They know what to do. They just want to get on and do it.

Hence, internally-inspired people do best with a lot of freedom. Whether they're designing an ad campaign or painting the boxroom, you'll get a better result if you stand well clear and give them space.

It's my party, and I'll cry if I want to. (Helen Shapiro, singer, on the joys of being internal)

So rather than dictating, present internals with two or three options. Rather than insisting, listen to their viewpoint. Rather than making them conform, offer support when they want to buck the trend. Above all, never, never, never challenge the inner voice that tells an internal what's right for them. Because when it comes to the crunch, if they have to choose, they will unhesitatingly follow the voice. Even if that means walking away from you.

One last warning about internals. They can be bad at celebration. They may simply not feel the need – because they don't share it. They provide their own internal round of applause, so they just fail to see that anyone else needs one.

I have a very dear external friend who needs serious celebration when she's completed a project. Meanwhile, her extremely internal other half can't see why she should want to do this.

So every time she clinches a business deal or finishes painting the kitchen, she's desperately in need of feedback – even just a hug to show that she's appreciated. He, meanwhile, often doesn't even remember to say well done to her – because as an internally-driven person, he doesn't feel the need.

Push me, pull you

 When it comes to maturity, being internal has a certain kudos. There is something very grown-up about internal attitudes to life – think 'self starting', 'she's her own woman' or Frank Sinatra's 'I did it My Way'.

But you need to be careful. There's a word for someone completely internal – and it's 'psychopath'. Internally-driven people can seem to just go their own way, oblivious to what their nearest and dearest – or their boss or their employees – want.

So if you're internally-inspired, for sure, be motivated by your own values and your own ethics, but also remember that one of the things that distinguishes humans from animals is our ability to deliberately take into account the people around us. So don't be wary if you find yourself influenced by others. Keep a notice on your desk (or your fridge): 'Taking feedback doesn't mean I'm a wimp.'

An internal may not be unaware of others, but they make their own decisions regardless (page 137).

If you want to become more externally-inspired
• Get others' input at the start of any task. Fresh ideas, varied suggestions, a new point of view – we're talking broadened horizons here. Don't panic; you don't have to accept everything – but at least listen and consider. Others have good ideas, so feel free to borrow.

                           what makes people tick?

- Check those around you are happy. This will not only create love in your life. It'll also improve your cashflow. One freelancer I know ends every professional communication with the phrase 'Tell me if you want anything more – or anything different.' She's not lost a client in three years.
- Listen politely if someone gives you negative feedback – and don't pull up the shutters. If more than two people give you the same piece of negative feedback, then fling the shutters wide. One criticism may be bitchiness but two or three is no coincidence.

All that said, if you're very externally-inspired, you'll also hit problems. Yes, you're socially competent because minute-to-minute you take on board what other people say to you. And in some ways you're wonderfully easy to live with because you're motivated to do what others want.

But the problem is that you may not be able to move a muscle without literally or mentally checking it out with your workmates, your favourite schoolteacher and the milkman. If someone criticizes you, you'll take it to heart needlessly. And – as explained before – if people you rate want different things for you or from you, you'll feel utterly torn in two.

Someone strongly external may be high on awareness of others (page 137).

For all these reasons, you may want to develop your more internally-driven side, to be slightly less influenced by others. Of course, as an external person, you'll feel uncomfortable even thinking about this – your inner voice will shriek 'that's selfish!' It isn't, though. Knowing your own mind makes you much easier for people to live with than being a reed in the wind.

If you want to become more internally-inspired
- Don't instantly go with every suggestion – take 'mulling' time. Particularly, check the feasibility of what people ask of you; given your external leanings, you'll be tempted to take on more

work than you can manage and try to do it more quickly than is humanly possible.

- Respect your inner mine detectors. One client, due to give a vital conference speech, came to me atypically gut-scared. She shrugged off her fears – but in fact, the conference politics backfired. 'I knew there was going to be trouble,' she said later. 'I should have trusted my own instincts.'
- Be receptive to feedback, of course. On the other hand, with your externally driven approach, you'll be tempted to take everything on board – however unrealistic. So get assertiveness training to help you spot when feedback is acceptable and when it's oppressive (see page 293).

External job, internal job

$ One of the most externally-inspired people I know is a designer who's been my friend for 20 years. If a client says 'jump', Jamie's only questions are 'how high and from which roof?'

And that makes him a superb commercial freelancer. He listens closely to what his clients want, fulfils their criteria, delivers just what's asked for. He's done so well that he has a studio on one of the most expensive and trendy streets in expensive, trendy London.

Then there's another friend, a sculptor. Peter's work is weird, wonderful, and more than slightly unnerving. He takes his own inner visions and translates them into wood. He claims never to have asked anyone whether his work is likeable or not – though it sells like hot cakes to people who appreciate it. Mind you, not everyone does appreciate it – but, of course, being an off-the-scale internal, Peter doesn't care!

Jamie is doing the best by other people. Peter is doing the best by himself. There's no way to compare them – and no point in doing so.

what makes people tick?

But there is a point in realizing that whilst both are in roughly the same line of business, the two men's motivations are completely different and that dictates the jobs they do. Peter would feel totally trapped if he had to constantly refer back to a client. Jamie, without his customers, simply wouldn't know what to do when he sat down at the drawing board every morning.

Good careers for internal people: lawyer, doctor, bookkeeper, entrepreneur, web designer, lecturer, inventor, writer, solo performer, motivational speaker.

If you're more internally-inspired, making your own day-to-day job decisions will be easy peasy – but you'll start to get edgy if asked to follow orders or meet outside requirements. So whatever field you're in, you need to be wary of roles where you work for demanding clients or heavy-handed management. Go for 'self-starter' jobs where you largely do your own thing.

Note I say largely, not entirely. Hardly any careers allow for total independence – you always need to take others' values and demands into account. Even as a freelancer, you have a straight choice. Handle the feedback or lose the work.

Good careers for external people: bank clerk, civil servant, flight attendant, retail assistant, telemarketeer, personal assistant, travel agent, recruitment consultant.

If you're more external, the career challenges will be different. What you need is a job situation that will give you the supervision you need and the support you want. So when scouring the job ads, look for the magic words 'human resources department', 'in-depth management' or 'regular appraisals'. Your disaster scenario is going to be any situation where you need to self-direct – working alone, self-employed or in a company with ineffective or laissez-faire leadership.

In extremis, if you're an external, set up your own motivation system or support group. As an external freelance writer, I get occasional 'feedback deprivation'; when I start to feel it bite, I call up a network of colleagues and mentors and ask for a few minutes 'tell me how I'm doing' time.

One final point: some jobs – particularly in the caring services – look as if they'll suit someone externally-driven. But actually, they're total minefields for anyone who isn't moderately internal or balanced between the two.

Counselling, is a good example. Sure you need to understand your unhappy and distressed clients. But you absolutely don't need to be motivated by them – because if you are, you'll get so hooked in to their unhappiness that you'll lose the very clarity and objectivity you need in order to help.

Danger alert

There's an interesting little variation on being internally-driven. It's called 'being strong-willed' – and it occurs when a lump of real distrust gets added to the mix.

This distrust might be down to someone having had a really hard time as a child – maybe having been bullied. So they end up incredibly wary that others are going to con them, do them down, take them over, control them. They aren't aware of this fear – to them it just seems that the world is a dangerous place and they need to protect themselves.

But the way they protect themselves is by becoming strong-willed. Quite simply, they dig their heels in. When someone tells them something or asks them to do something, their gut reaction isn't 'interesting ... I didn't know that ... sure, why not?' but 'why are you saying this? ... why do I need to know it? ... why on earth should I do it?'

what makes people tick?

And, to be blunt, this little personality subpattern can make people hell on wheels, both professionally and personally. At work, their default option may be to question reports, resist recommendations, make waves against the management. At home, they may bristle at their partner's every suggestion or request, start arguments over the smallest of things, query an inaccurate comment or a tentative suggestion.

Want to know where you fall on this scale? See page 284.

Strong-willed people are the ones who'll struggle for days trying to programme their new mobile – and when they turn in despair to the manual, will still feel patronized. They're the ones who'll park on the double yellow line just to be awkward – and if booked, will run their own defence in court!

How do you deal with such a one? Most fundamentally, give them respect. Because the upside of such incredible strong will is incredible single mindedness. For a project, they'll keep going until they fall over. For a friendship, they'll go the extra mile – or ten. And if they decide to commit to a relationship, they'll hang in 'til death us do part'. No surrender.

Six tips for handling a 'strong-willed' personality

- Don't front up or become aggressive. Strong will has its basis in fear, so anything you can do to reassure, prove qualifications or make it clear that you're not trying to control the other person will help them realize they can trust you.
- Do give genuine appreciation – if you tell a strong-willed person that you rate them (or if they're your partner, that you love them), they're more likely to relax and start to listen.
- Don't, however, knuckle under or placate – every apology will make a strong-willed person more convinced that there's something to be wary of. Be quietly confident and their confidence in you will rise.
- Do suggest, hint, plant ideas, discuss, invite contributions, get them interested and involved.

external/internal inspiration strategy

- Don't pressure, nag, threaten, manipulate. The more your emotions rise, the more a strong-willed person will simply dig their heels in.
- Do consider walking away. If a client or colleague is never open to suggestions, avoid dealing with them. If a partner says no to every single request, consider ending the relationship.

And what if, having read this far, you start feeling waves of self-recognition flooding over you. You have to admit that you do sometimes dig your heels in – and your spouse (or workmates, or friends) sometimes do accuse you of stubbornness. You wouldn't want to admit it, but you just might be strong-willed. What should you do about that?

Three tips for a strong-willed personality
- Don't feel bad about it. Yes, you may get people's backs up. But there's nothing wrong with being strong-willed in a world where compliance gets you disregarded, oppressed and sometimes enslaved.
- Remember what strong-willed people contribute. It was George Bernard Shaw who said, quite rightly, 'A reasonable man adapts himself to the world around him. An unreasonable man expects the world to adapt to him. Therefore, all progress is made by unreasonable men.'
- But if being strong-willed is making you or others in your life unhappy, then go on an assertiveness course (see page 293). Don't panic – such courses won't ask you to compromise your principles or lay yourself open to hassle. They will teach you ways of negotiating what you want without alienating other people.

what makes people tick?

PS: Avoiding power struggles

When working with any group, identify the strong-willed ones early on and get them on-side. The quick and dirty way to do this is to set everyone a simple starter task – like reading through the hand-out or arranging the chairs. He who hesitates is strong-willed.

After that, target the more internally-inspired ones by appealing to their individual values – a sense of fair play, a desire to achieve.

Once the majority are supporting you, the externally-inspired members of the group will happily follow the party line.

HOW PERSONALITY WORKS 5

You move in lots of life contexts. You go to work. You go and play. You stay at home. You drive around. You meet your partner. You spend time with the children. You visit your family. You curl up alone …

In each context, personality's slightly different. For example …

- **Your personality may vary because you've only got a certain amount of a personality pattern to go round. You're so proactive at work that at home you have no energy for action - and come over all reactive.**
- **Your personality may vary because you've learned to be different people in different settings. You're motivated 'towards' in sport because you've always done well - so aim for higher and higher goals. But you're motivated 'away-from' in relationships because you've often been dumped - so you constantly try to avoid failure.**
- **Your personality may vary because different things are expected of you in different contexts. You have to be an organized judger at work because you'd lose your job if you weren't. But your friends are a laid back bunch and so you're a relaxed perceiver when you hang out with them.**
- **Your personality may vary because you change contexts. Move jobs and you'll turn into an achiever because everyone else in the firm is. Move relationships and you'll turn all pessimistic because your partner's so optimistic that you don't need to be.**

Personality isn't consistent. It alters according to the context you're in.

Wanna be in my gang?
Group interaction style

18 In a group, what kind of bonds do we like? This personality pattern looks at what sort of interaction we feel most comfortable with and how much autonomy we need to have.

Do we get on with things by ourselves? Or do we like to be alongside others the whole time? Have other people around only when we need them? Whether it's a project at work or doing the dishes at home, how far do we need to do things ourselves? And how much do we depend on team spirit to keep us going?

More independent

An independent's always much happier working alone. When it comes to getting things done, independents know their job – and they don't want anyone else interfering.

So at work, they love being told that this project is 'theirs', that it's all down to them. They hate being told that they've got to consult, take others into account – or, horror of horrors, wait for others to perform before they themselves can get on. An independent would rather be strung up by their thumbs than serve on a committee.

Want to know your own group interaction style? See page 285.

If the independent at work is also an independent at home, then they'll love solo hobbies – surfing the web, hang-gliding or that most independent of activities, fishing. Even on the dance floor, independents fight shy of anything demanding competition or cooperation; lose the ballroom dancing, instead they'll mark out their own space and get into their own movements.

For an example of a serious independent across all life contexts, take one of my oldest friends. He's a committed humanist, genuinely believes people are the most important thing in life and has a close circle of friends. But for the past 30 years since leaving Oxford University, he's worked as a freelance programmer on contract, his only client contact a meeting every six months or so for briefing and feedback.

An independent tends to be internally-inspired (page 151).

On a weekend? On weekends, he has an immense list of flora and fauna that he wants to see – so he sets off up mountains. By himself. Of course.

More team-playing

Three things are important when a team player's working – support, support and support.

At work, their catchphrase is 'all for one and one for all'. They love meetings and conferences and insist that everything is talked through until they reach consensus. Put them outside the peer group – either working on their own or as a manager and therefore not one of the lads – and they fade away. But round the table envelope-stuffing is team-player heaven!

Someone who's a team player outside work will tend to want to do things in groups. They'll love the team hug after a goal or the high that happens when people buckle down and help with a charity event or getting a street party off the ground.

A team player tends to be externally-inspired (page 151).

British writer and ideas genius Douglas Adams – of *Hitchhiker's Guide to the Galaxy* fame – was an over-the-top team player. And his big career break as a radio scriptwriter played to that strength. Because writing comedy scripts involves talking absolutely everything through with others on the team – over and over again until it's right.

Douglas blossomed under that regime. When it brought him the stunning success of *Hitchhiker's Guide,* however, the natural next step was to turn his hand to writing novels.

Big mistake. The life of a lone writer was Douglas's worst nightmare. The brilliance was still in his head – but without people to support him, the brilliance stayed there and he became a legend in his own time for missing deadlines because of unshiftable writer's block. On one occasion his editor simply moved in with him, holding his hand on a daily basis until the book got done!

More proximity

A proximity person straddles the two arenas: independent and team. They want their own bag but not completely alone. They want to have others round them, but not be beholden. Sure a proximity person is happy to share ideas and energy on a big project; but they'll throw a total wobbly if asked to share authority and control on their personal piece.

You can probably see where this is going in a work context. Given confidence and competence, proximity is the personality subpattern of a manager, someone self-sufficient enough to take charge and head up a group, yet open to group feedback and support. With time, promotion – and a few good training courses – people with this profile often end up in charge.

In an out-of-work context too, proximity people will want a mix of 'with' and 'alone'. They'll be happy joining in as part of a family and social group – but they do like to be left to get on with what they know they can do best.

A good example of proximity was provided by the cox of one of the big British rowing squads. (The cox, in case you don't know, is the person who shouts from the front of the boat as opposed to the hulking great athletes who do the business in the rest of the boat.) This guy confessed to me that he loved the sport and the job he did, but he wasn't really a team player.

Excuse me? Isn't rowing totally a team game – everyone working together, in harmony. Yeeeees, he said uncertainly – but the real

A proximity person is often balanced between externally and internally-inspired (page 151).

team stuff was done by the lads, rowing in synch stroke after stroke. He liked to be up the end on his own, responsible for his own bit, not one of the crowd. He even admitted that when they all went down to the pub after practice, he didn't hang in there long. A few quick halves and then he'd slope off home.

20% of people tend to be independent, 20% of people tend to be team, 60% of people tend to be proximity.

Mix and match

People can combine these three subpatterns – usually in specific contexts. So at home, they may be strongly team – doing things together as a family. In leisure time, they may be independent – trotting off to indulge their passion for drawing or playing the guitar. At work, they may be a proximity manager – wanting their own area of responsibility.

It's rare to find someone who balances all these roles equally in a single context. But last year, I met one of the few. My chiropractor

Independent.

Team.

Proximity.

what makes people tick?

works as an independent when he's seeing clients one-on-one. But he's also part of a team practice that has group meetings every month. And two days a week, he lectures at the local Uni – in a proximity role with his own area of expertise, but working alongside colleagues. A talented man.

A final point: as with so many personality subpatterns, the one people score lowest on is also interesting – and churns up a variety of positive and negative feelings. Low on independence? That may mean someone who literally seizes up when asked to work entirely on their own – and may well be slightly scathing about or very envious of those who can.

Low on team-playing? This person's likely to be uncomfortable with group decision making – and either regard those who need team support as being weak or envy their social competence.

Low on proximity? The discomfort here is going to be about taking charge. So low-proximity people will hold back from a management role – but at heart may wish they were up to it. And that means they may look admiringly across at the leaders of this world – or be suspicious and resistant to them. If there's a heckler in the audience or a rebel in the group, you're probably looking at a low-proximity (but wannabe) person.

Loving a loner

'It is a truth universally acknowledged, that a single man in possession of a good fortune must be in want of a wife.' (Jane Austen) ♥

But not if he's an independent. Sure, today we tend to think there's something weird about a person who's not in a long-term relationship. But there may be a less damning explanation. He (or more rarely she) may be an off-the-scale independent.

Because when it comes to the crunch, your independent won't actually want to share the day-to-day organization of his existence with someone else. He much prefers to run his home, his work, his social life to his own specifications, thank you very much. No live-in lovers need apply.

Which has some interesting ramifications for you if you want him. In short, be wary. However much he cares, however convinced you are that you can domesticate him, hold back. Or go find yourself a nice willing team player instead. Or live separately – celebrity Toyah Wilcox and her husband Robert Fripp spend an average of only two months of the year together and it suits them very nicely thank you. My bet is that they're both independents.

This joke just about sums it up. An architect, an artist and a programmer are discussing whether it's better to have a wife or a mistress.

Says the architect 'I just love spending time with my wife, building a solid foundation for our relationship'.

'Nah ...' says the artist. 'I prefer having a mistress, because of the great sex.'

The IT guy disagrees, 'I want both'. 'Both?' 'Yeah. If you have a wife and a mistress, they each assume you're spending time with the other woman. Then you can go to the office and get some work done.'

Now, there's your classic independent!

When you need to get a job done

$ Work with someone and you'll always be wise to respect their group interaction style. Because try to get even the most socially
♥ competent independent working as part of a team and you'll get tears and tantrums. And leave even the most introvert of team players to work on their own and they'll feel abandoned and betrayed.

How to manage an independent

- Do give credit where it's due – they may not always be coopera-tive, but they are stunningly self-sufficient.
- Do get them to inform you what they're doing, when they'll do it by and what they need from you. Otherwise they'll just do their own thing.
- Tell them often that they have control over things, choice in what they do.
- Don't badger them to be 'part of the group' or try to give team appraisals.
- Close to home: never cook with an independent – they'll begin by sharpening their elbows and end up throwing knives.
- If this is you, give yourself permission to have total control over what you do. Choose jobs that leave you free to make your own decisions. And choose a partner who doesn't wobble when you need to go off and work on your own projects.

How to manage a team player

- Do give credit where it's due – they may not always be self-sufficient, but they are incredibly supportive.
- Do give formal briefing and debriefings and lots of support for what they're doing.
- Tell them often how valuable they are to their colleagues, the department, the company, the family.
- Don't expect them to work alone or in the lead.
- Close to home: if a team player's doing the ironing, pop your head round the door every few minutes to offer moral support.
- If this is you, give yourself permission to actively seek out others to work with. Choose jobs with a clear cooperative bias, in companies with strong team culture and be upfront about your need for group support. And choose a partner who, when you get stuck, has the will and skill to support you to move on.

A team player tends to be 'your rules for you, your rules for me' (page 176).

How to manage a proximity person

A proximity person tends to be 'my rules for me, my rules for you' (page 176).

- Do give credit where it's due – they may not always be biddable, but they are leadership material.
- Do create a balance – give them something to do that's theirs ... but with enough support to keep them going.
- Don't undermine them by querying their judgement – they need to feel trusted.
- Tell them often what is their responsibility, but also how other people support and back them.
- Close to home: if you value the crockery, never try to tell a proximity how to do the washing up.
- If this is you, give yourself permission to take the lead on things without holding back. Choose jobs where you can have your own responsibilities and aim to move fairly quickly into management. Choose a partner who'll be happy if you take charge, at least sometimes.

Lastly, when it comes to your own group interaction style, work with your grain rather than against it. One of my friends, a heavy-duty team player, keeps trying to pass as an independent. He feels it's more grown-up to work for himself – so four times over the past decade he's set up as a freelance consultant.

But each time, within weeks, he seems to end up hiring a stream of so-called 'admin assistants', who've no actual work to do, but whose role is to be the 'team' he needs to keep him going. And each time, his over-employment results in a cash flow crisis and then he has to rein in, sack the entire staff and start all over again.

If only he could see that it would be easier – and kinder to his despairing accountant – if he simply gave in and got a job in a multinational.

PS: Working the gender divide

Women are more likely to be team players. Men are more likely to be independents or proximity people. And like it or not, what this means is that men will typically opt out of groups or move to take control, whilst women will typically hang in there with groups and end up giving team support.

If you're facilitating a group, then for an easy life, get the men leading and the women following. But it's more empowering and developmental for individuals and for society alike to challenge the women to lead and the men to give support.

My rules or yours?
Group standards model

(19) Get any group of people together and there have to be rules. Not formal rules, like laws, edicts or legislations. No, we're talking principles here. We're talking standards. We're talking about the way we think the world ought to work.

From the temperature we think beer ought to be to how monogamous we feel relationships ought to be (completely or not at all?). Everyone, even if they're a total rebel, has an idea of the rules of engagement. And, everyone has an idea of whether these rules should vary from person to person.

This personality pattern explores whether we're more likely to feel that everyone should follow our standards or more likely to believe in 'horses for courses' and 'live and let live'.

My rules for me, my rules for you

Want to know your own group standards style? See page 288.

If we believe 'my rules for me, my rules for you,' then we're clear about our own principles – and we want other people to live by them. We believe everyone's basically the same, so everyone does – and should – think, feel and act more or less the same. Off-the-scale, we're talking people who believe that everyone needs to knuckle under. The words 'dogmatist', 'dictator', 'Spanish Inquisition' come inexorably to mind.

Take a more normal and less freaky version of this, though, and it's understandable. Most of us believe that other people are like we are, following the rules we do. And therefore we expect them to toe our line. As a result, if they don't, we can get confused, judgemental or antagonistic.

what makes people tick?

One of most interesting examples of this I've ever come across was a woman I knew at college. Heavily into studying in her first year, she gave the rest of us grief because we didn't keep our noses to the grindstone. A few weeks into her second year, however, she discovered partying – after which, if you weren't out there with her every weekend, she let you know about it. Then just before Easter, she found lurvvv ... and within weeks of the engagement ring being on her finger, she was wondering aloud why the rest of us didn't calm down and settle down.

It wasn't that she wanted to give us all a hard time. It was just that whatever Carole was doing, she genuinely believed was best for the world.

My rules for me, your rules for you

If we believe 'my rules for me, your rules for you', we're clear about our own principles – and completely laid back about others living by theirs. We believe 'it takes all sorts to make a world' and that everyone should 'live and let live'.

We're liberal. We're tolerant. We don't judge. We're lovely to be around because we take people as they come.

But if asked for our opinion, we may be less than helpful – because we deeply believe that what we do is not necessarily what anyone else should do. And that means that if advice or support is needed, we may feel at a loss, unable to suggest, guide or direct because we literally don't feel it's any of our business.

Ironically, the only time a 'my rules for me, your rules for you' person may feel that others ought to follow their example is when it comes to tolerance. Because if we run this personality pattern, we tend to feel uncomfortable and critical about people who don't run it. A 'my rules for me, your rules for you' person, normally the most placid soul, will become frustrated and angry beyond measure at intolerance, prejudice and dictatorship.

Your rules for you, your rules for me

If we believe 'your rules for you, your rules for me', then we're happy to accept other people's principles – they seem just as valid, if not more valid, than our own.

This may be because we're not quite sure of our own rules and tend to adopt other people's. Maybe we're young and haven't yet formed our own standards. Or we lack confidence and daren't form our own standards. Or we're naturally externally inspired (see page 151), so we like to please others by adopting their standards.

Or, we're in an unfamiliar situation. Most of us flip into 'your rules for you, your rules for me' when on holiday in a completely foreign country or during the first week in a new job. We look around, see how others are holding their chopsticks – or what they do when they take their tea break. And we do it their way.

At its best, 'your rules for you, your rules for me' means we can adapt easily to new circumstances, because we aren't clinging on to what we know. We learn easily, adjust happily and conform. At its worst, we find it hard to make our own decisions. And, we're very easily led. Cults seize happily on 'your rules for you, your rules for me' people because, quite simply, they're a total walkover.

Mix and match

It's unusual to find people mixing these personality components in a single context, varying the subpatterns they run within a single arena such as work or home.

But it's very common to find people running one subpattern in one context, another subpattern in another context. So they're laid back about what a partner does, but insist on employees following every regulation. (And quite right too – in a work context, it's appropriate for the managers to run 'my rules for me, my rules for you' and employees to run 'your rules for you, your rules for me'.)

My rules for me,
my rules for you.

My rules for me,
your rules for you.

Your rules for you,
your rules for me.

The supreme example of rules contextualization in action can be found within the British counselling network, the Samaritans. Founded to lend a listening ear, the Samaritans has a huge team of volunteers at the end of the telephone line 24/7, to listen to those who need them.

Now, in their everyday lives, these volunteers may run a variety of personality patterns. They'll almost certainly include a great deal of 'my rules for me, my rules for you' – particularly if they are parents and need to firmly enforce standards on errant offspring!

But when they start a shift at the Samaritans, however, all bets are off. Quite simply, Samaritans' volunteers completely put to one side 'my rules for me, my rules for you' and wholeheartedly adopt 'my rules for me, your rules for you'. Because never once do they tell the distressed clients on the other end of the phone that they 'should' be living their lives differently. Instead – even if the person on the other end of the phone chooses suicide – it is part of a Samaritans' commitment to support without criticism.

It's an awesome example of 'my rules for me, your rules for you' carried through to its courageous conclusion.

Danger – rules at work

$ When a person with one rules subpattern works with – or for – a person with a different rules subpattern, things get interesting.

My rules for me, my rules for you

Work for a 'my rules for me, my rules for you' person and, naturally enough, they'll expect you to follow the rules – their personal rules, management's rules, company's rules ... Problem is, because they think those rules are universal, they may not tell you what those rules actually are. So particularly when you first meet them and are getting a sense of their standards, ask them to spell out everything – then do your best to comply.

Manage someone like this and you'll need to make sure that they agree with the rules you're laying down. And where there are conflicts between what you as a manager demand and what they think is right, then expect hassle. They'll try to convince you that you ought to change your mind. And if they're convincing enough – and you're flexible enough – you may find yourself following their lead instead of them following yours.

Appoint someone like this as a manager and they'll be fine, at ease when enforcing standards on others. Just make sure it's the company's standards they're enforcing, not just their own.

My rules for me, your rules for you

Work for a 'my rules for me, your rules for you' person and you'll love the fact that they never give you a hard time. But you may well

what makes people tick?

hate the fact that they never seem to tell you what to do – and if you ask for guidelines, they get confused because the question doesn't make sense to them. You'll need to go above their heads or to a more clued-up colleague to get any idea of 'the deal' in your team, office or company.

Manage someone like this and whilst they'll be happy with you doing your thing, they'll also want to do theirs. They may actually be uncontrollable; prepare for quiet rebellion.

And if you appoint someone like this as a manager, you'll rue the day. Quite simply, you'll find it impossible to insist that they insist – they won't be able to tell others what to do, because they don't think it's their place.

Your rules for you, your rules for me

Work for, or with, or manage a 'your rules for you, your rules for me' person and you'll find them very open to your views. They'll think your ideas are just as valid as theirs – more so, in fact, because they don't have many of their own.

But don't appoint someone like this as a manager, because they won't have a clear sense of standards. In fact, they may come across as quite weak, shifting their principles – and sometimes their ethics and morals – with the wind. So never rely on them to stand up and be counted; they'll take their lead from what the majority does.

Rules of engagement

The fact that most of us are 'my rules for me, my rules for you' people can create some interesting glitches in relationships.

Think about it. You believe that the way 'things should be done' is the way everyone thinks things should be done. The problem is, your partner thinks the same. Not only may the two of you have rules that differ, but you may not realize you have to check out the ways in which they differ.

So you feel, deep down, that a relationship should mean you spend the majority of your free time together. Your partner believes that, once committed, you should both use the relationship as a secure launch pad – spending some time together but by no means all.

But you don't tell each other. And then your expectations clash. And then there are rows. The answer, quite simply, is to check out and keep checking. Don't assume, because your rules seem like the right ones, that your partner shares them. Talk about it. Swap notes. Get clear what the 'rules' for you as a couple are.

The ideas I stand for aren't mine. I borrowed them from Socrates. I swiped them from Chesterfield. I stole them from Jesus. (Dale Carnegie, proud of running 'your rules for you, your rules for me')

If you do this and continue to do this, then with time you'll learn to blend your ideals and standards – and the friction will disappear. Like many successful long-term couples, you may actually move to a variation which reads something like 'our rules for us, our rules for everyone else' – feeling that your mutual standards and principles are the right ones and everyone should do things your way.

And there can also be a neat little twist on the scenario. Because one person can take things a stage further and start to run 'your rules for you, your rules for me' with their partner. In other words, they take on board their partner's standards rather than their own.

Acceptance of prevailing standards often means we have no standards of our own. (Jean Toomer, US author and poet, criticizing people who run 'your rules for you, your rules for me')

what makes people tick?

Sometimes this works superbly. I lost track of a college friend for a few years because he'd moved away from our set and into a heavy drugs scene. And the last I'd heard, he was hitting the hard stuff. But then I bumped into him, with his new girlfriend Hazel and a few other mutual friends. Paul was happy, well dressed and obviously had his life together. When he was out of earshot, I buttonholed one of the others. 'What on earth happened for Paul to get clean?' I muttered. There was a knowing wink. 'Hazel happened ...' was the reply.

But this taking on of your partner's 'rules' can backfire. If you take them on board regardless of whether they're really right for you, then in time you can feel you're living a lie. (Not to mention the problems that can arise if your partner's way of life is potentially risky. What would have happened if instead of Paul starting to take on Hazel's rules of living, Hazel had started taking on Paul's?)

There's a footnote to all this. What happens when you fall out of love? Well, that's when it can get nasty. Over time, if love fades, you revert to your original default option, 'my rules for me, my rules for you'. And then you start feeling upset, angry and betrayed because your partner doesn't do things the way you like. Outraged that they don't, you start asking. Then nagging. Then demanding. Then pressuring. And, of course, so does your partner.

That way lies madness. Or more likely, divorce.

PS: Instant diagnosis 3

Two questions will sort out who runs which rule subpattern.

First ask about any simple choice, 'What do you think you should do?' Anyone who runs any variation of 'my rules for me' will be able to answer – and if they're confused, don't know or rely entirely on your advice, then they run 'your rules for me'.

Then ask 'What do you think I should do?' Anyone who runs any variation of 'my rules for you' will be able to answer and if they bounce the question back to you and seem unable to give you counsel, then they run 'your rules for you'.

Get the two components, combine them, and you'll know the complete pattern that this person runs.

How hard do you bite back?
Satir's conflict categories

20 Say there's some variety of group interpersonals. A disagreement, a problem, a conflict, a crisis … What's our fallback position? On the defensive? On the attack? Sliding out of the front line? Or freezing under fire? American therapist Virginia Satir identified a personality pattern – consisting of five separate subpatterns – that comes to the surface when things get tough.

Placating

Step on a placator's foot and she'll be the one to apologize. Because placators know that peacemakers get blessed – or at least don't get trashed. And so a typical placator will soothe, please and pacify.

She – for placators are usually female – will feel uncomfortable fighting back, so she'll rarely disagree – even if she's being criticized. And she'll typically back down – even if it's her victory. She'll actually agree when somebody blames her – because that's the easiest option.

Her aim is to get others to be nice to her – and, as placators tend to be externally-inspired (page 151), she'll therefore probably go with whatever the other person wants. She'll hold eye contact, smile a lot, nonverbally ask forgiveness. Her mantra at work, home and play is 'Sorreeeee'.

Want to know your own conflict style? See page 290.

Blaming

If a blamer steps on someone's foot, he'll expect *them* to apologize. Because a blamer's classic default is to shift the responsibility – and there are sooooo many lovely ways of doing this.

He can nag, he can sulk, he can shout, he can hit out. Or he can pretend that it's not a problem and then launch a surprise attack a few hours later when everyone thinks the worst is over.

Lately, I've noticed our entire society running this subpattern: the new breed of 'Sue 'em and run' law firms base their entire turnover on that philosophy. My latest sighting was a catchy little TV jingle that runs 'where there's blame, there's a claim!'

Distracting

Did she step on someone's foot? Nah. A distractor will claim she wasn't even there. She'll smile, crack a joke, say what lovely weather it is today, do everything but turn cartwheels in order to deflect attention.

And she'll come into her own in the work context, where it's not quite so acceptable to do the sort of heavy duty blaming and placating that is acceptable in private life, among friends, family and lovers. So if an employee isn't pulling her weight or otherwise messing up, her preferred option is often a bit of distracting on the side. Her favourite phrase? 'It wasn't me'.

Computing

When a computer steps on someone's foot, he simply won't register the fact. He – for computers are usually male – is the one who just doesn't seem to feel anything, doesn't respond emotionally to what's happened. He simply shuts down on feelings – not to mention tending to downgrade the other person's pain by suggesting

what makes people tick?

Placator. Blamer. Distracter Computer. Leveller.

ten logical reasons why they're over-reacting. Think Mr Spock in *Star Trek*.

A clarification: a computer may seem like he's responding calmly to a crisis. Not so. He does feel – he's panicking just as much as anyone else. But he's trying to handle that panic by cutting himself off at the neck. And actually, that's just as bad an idea as placating, blaming or distracting, because he's missing out on the information or motivation his body is trying to give him.

So he'll act, but over-rationally. He'll respond, but unresponsively. The computer's the person who explains – clearly, logically and calmly – why homicide was really the only option he had.

Men are more likely to blame: 92% of horn tooting at lights is done by men. 96% of burglaries are carried out by men. 88% of murders are committed by men.

Levelling

A leveller who steps on someone's foot will notice. Then she'll move back. Then she'll ask if there's anything she can do. She won't grovel, dump or look the other way – and she won't cut off from her feelings. She'll be genuinely regretful – but unlike people who run the other four personality subpatterns, she won't go into a spiral of defensive responses.

So a leveller is going to be the one to hang in there under stress or in conflict and simply get things sorted. She will strike a balance between thinking and feeling – and that means that she will both face up logically to the problem and have the emotional energy to sort it out. Whether at home or away, she'll have the space to listen to other people, take into account everyone's needs and find a solution.

Anyone who works with a leveller, marries a leveller or has a leveller for a friend therefore has an easy life. And anyone who is a leveller should make sure that their colleagues, spouses and friends are duly grateful!

You're like this because ...

 So someone's a placator, a blamer, a computer, a distractor, a leveller – or even a bit of all five. But why are they? What is it that determines someone's conflict category?

It's actually all down to what happens when a person is young. Because a child picks up whatever they see happening around them. So if parents, family, teachers or friends have a particular conflict subpattern, the child is liable to develop it too. In particular, he or she will tend to copy their same gender parent or the adult most identified with. So father was a blamer, mother a placator: if the child is close to Dad, she'll grow up blaming for her country; close to Mum and she'll placate for the world.

what makes people tick?

Women are least likely to be computers; 65–75% of women prefer to feel rather than think.

Another way things might go is this. A particular approach to conflict works for a child and they hang on to that with enthusiasm. So if a winning smile twisted people round a child's finger, then she may end up as a woman who uses that smile to placate. Or if hiding feelings helped a teenager to fend off the bullies at school, then he may end up as a man who cuts off from emotion in a computer-like way.

The final determining element is this. The more stable, accepting and empowering a child's upbringing is, the less likely they are to run any of the more annoying and self-destructive subpatterns – the more likely they are to cope with crisis and stress calmly and effectively. The bottom line is that the more positive your upbringing, the more likely you are to be a leveller.

Learning to level

Being a heavy-duty placator, blamer, computer or distractor isn't a massively good idea. That's pretty obvious. Not only do these personality subpatterns feel uncomfortable to run, none will exactly get you brownie points with your boss, your mates or your nearest and dearest.

Of course, everyone runs a bit of the four more unhelpful personality subpatterns. But the aim should always be to shift your behaviour towards helpful 'levelling'. Here's how.

If you tend to be a placator
- you may think it's a good subpattern as it seems to smooth things over

- in fact, you won't get what you want – plus you can drive people crazy by always apologizing
- instead, to move towards being a leveller, learn not to be wary of other people's disapproval
- take action: assertiveness training will help you learn to cope with conflict clearly and effectively. Your local college or adult education centre will probably run a course. For further resources, also see page 293.

If you tend to be a blamer
- you may think it's a good subpattern because at least no one shouts at you
- in fact, it alienates people – plus by shifting responsibility, you give away your power
- instead, to move towards being a leveller, learn that the world's not out to get you and that temper tantrums don't work
- take action: anger management skills will help you to stay calm and approachable and avoid stirring up conflict. For further resources, see page 293.

If you tend to be a distractor
- you may think it's a good subpattern because it gets you off the hook
- in fact, you never get to face problems – plus you never take responsibility for things
- instead, to move towards being a leveller, learn to face it when other people gripe; then either take their criticisms on board or stand firm in believing you're OK
- take action: confidence training will help you stand up for yourself or admit you're not doing well and help you to ask for support. For further resources, see page 293.

what makes people tick?

If you tend to be a computer

- you may think it's a good subpattern because it keeps you clear of messy emotion
- in fact, you miss out by ignoring feelings – plus you may come across as hard-hearted
- instead, to move towards being a leveller, allow yourself to pay more attention to what others are feeling and take their emotions into account
- take action: a personal development course such as co-counselling will help you become more at ease with your feelings. For further resources, see page 293.

Conflict of roles

In the year 2000, the Wimbledon men's final was between six times' champion Pete Sampras and Australian Pat Rafter.

Afterwards, Rafter reported that during the match he'd 'choked' – been overcome by emotion. He was nervous at playing in front of a crowd of 14,000, intimidated by Sampras, excited at the thought of winning – above all, he was fired up by the sheer battle on Centre Court. So his physiology went into overdrive – blood pressure soaring, adrenalin pumping, heart rate 200 beats per minute.

Now, it wasn't clear, particularly to Rafter, just what this Centre Court conflict was doing to his brain – making him blame, placate, compute or distract. But it sure as anything wasn't allowing him to hit the ball with a level head and a sure hand.

To have in general but little feeling, seems to be the only security against feeling too much on any particular occasion. (British writer George Eliot extolling the virtues of being a computer)

Sampras on the other hand did hit the ball that way. He didn't panic, didn't get fired up, but neither did he switch off – he was fully engaged physically and mentally throughout the match. It wasn't just that he's been there six times before. It's also that when it comes to tennis, Pete Sampras is a natural born leveller.

No marks for guessing who won the match.

What this means for you and your career is this. If you're a leveller, you can probably do any job, however pressured it is and deal with the stress involved. But if you have a very high score in any of the other Satir subpatterns, then don't take jobs where there's emotional pressure, particularly conflict. Like Rafter, you'll choke – and end up not only a miserable bunny, but also a failing one.

So don't do aggro jobs, ones with lots of credit control or stroppy clients. Because if you're a placator, you'll end up taking all the blame and being walked over. If you're a computer, you'll just retreat into paralysis. If you blame or distract, then you'll run your number and alienate a lot of people. And in all four cases, you'll probably overeat, never sleep or develop a set of stress-related ailments.

Instead, opt for easier-going jobs and nonstressful work environments – at least until you've learned to be much, much more of a leveller.

Disarming the enemy

So there's a crisis, a disagreement, a fight. How do you cope with other people's Satir categories?

Sure, levellers are great – they'll keep their heads, stay in touch with their hearts, talk things through to a win-win conclusion. But how do you handle the other, less user-friendly personality subpatterns?

The thing to realize is that all four – even the seemingly hard-hearted 'computer' – are signs that a person is feeling bad. They may be stressed. They may feel under siege. They want help.

So it just won't work if you add more negative emotion to the pot. Criticism, sarcasm, mockery or shouting will simply give the other person more to feel bad about – and then they'll just up the ante – placating, blaming, distracting or cutting off at the neck. Instead, you need to lower the threat level and allow things to chill.

If you can't convince them, confuse them. (American President Harry S. Truman recommending a distractor approach)

How? With someone you're close to – a friend or partner – the best approach is almost always just to give them space. Given undivided attention and a large box of paper hankies. Almost anyone will ultimately calm down, start thinking clearly and start behaving more like a leveller.

This may not seem easy if you're rowing with your partner at 2am – and of course, if you regularly row with your partner at 2am, then this book won't help; you need a couples counsellor. But if someone close to you loses their rag or suffers a trauma or crisis, then simply listen to them; given your support, they'll find their own way through the emotions and come up shining on the other side.

('Computer' people, by the way, don't need the paper hankies; they'll simply sit quietly and pretend the emotional pain isn't happening. But if you can let them feel supported, then they will in the end start feeling and thinking again, operating on a human rather than a computer level.)

If supporting strong emotion isn't appropriate – with clients, colleagues, employees – then the best way to lower the aggro level is to get everyone to take a break. Studies by American psychologist John Gottman suggest that a minimum of 20 minutes is about the right time span for a 'cooldown' break. Say 'go think about it' or 'why don't we have a coffee'.

After that, run a more targeted campaign to meet the particular personality subpattern you're dealing with.

- A placator is chiefly scared of your disapproval, so give reassurance. Find some way to tell them they're fine, an 'ideal client', 'brilliant colleague'. They'll soon chill out and be more able to think clearly.
- A blamer has a deep fear of being blamed themselves – so blaming in return will only stoke the flames. And steer them away from blaming comments about third parties – instead, get them defining what exactly the problem is and what can be done about it.
- A distractor will try to divert your attention. So don't fall for long explanations, excuses or reasons 'why' the crisis arose. Instead, ask direct, 'closed' questions – ones to which the answers are 'yes' or 'no' – in order to get clear what is happening and move things on.
- A computer will simply freeze and stop thinking. Once they've chilled out however, their brains will click into gear and you can get them running the same mental approach that works with a blamer. Ask factual questions, make practical suggestions, create an action plan – get a solution.

If an American is hit on the head by a ball, he sues. If a Japanese is hit, he says, 'It's my fault'. (Koji Yanese of the Japan Federation of Bar Association on blamers and placators)

what makes people tick?

PS: Refereeing a row

If a group argument develops, this is an effective approach.

First get any levellers on side by making a clear statement of what you need in order to find a solution.

Then appeal to the computers by asking them to think things through.

Meanwhile, ask directly for calm and supportive behaviour from the group – that will pull the placators and distractors in.

By this time, the blamers will stick out like sore thumbs because they're the only ones still causing trouble. Tell them you'll deal with their concerns later, in private (where you can defuse their anger much more effectively).

Using personality secrets to ... read other people

21 Almost certainly, one of the reasons you bought this book was to understand other people better. You may want to understand people you know and love – partner, relative, friend. You may want to understand people you know but don't love – the relative from hell or the stroppy colleague. You may want to get some sort of handle on people you're meeting for the first time – neighbours, clients, a new boss. Will this book help you?

It will. You'll need to know the basic patterns outlined in the main body of the book. But once you have that knowledge, you can use it to interpret what others are doing and start to understand who they are. And then you can work with that.

Here's a small but real example. I once went along with a friend who had to take a pair of jeans back to an extremely upmarket store. The jeans had shrunk – badly – and she wanted them changed. Now, we both presupposed that the assistant's basic motivation was affiliation – sales assistants' usual incentive. So my friend went in friendly, all smiles and warm, soft voice tones, asking nicely for what she wanted.

It's pattern extremes that really affect things, influence people's approach to life. So spot the extremes and leave the normal traits to look after themselves.

Wrong. The assistant was not motivated by affiliation. In fact, he argued. Got all curt to show he wasn't impressed by anyone's friendly manner. And from that evidence, my friend concluded that

what makes people tick?

the guy was not – in that context at any rate – an affiliator. Message received and understood.

And message acted on. Because, knowing that she wasn't dealing with an affiliator, my friend decided to try another tack – and, basing her guess on the fact that this was a very upmarket store, she surmised that the man's motivation was achievement.

So she lost her smile. Got all serious. Reminded the assistant firmly that his store was the most prestigious in town and that she expected better service. Instant shift in sales assistant. He replaced the item immediately, hoping that we'd 'continue to shop here in future'. To him, what mattered was not being liked, but being best.

For more about motivator modes, see page 5.

Knowing about personality meant my friend could understand that assistant. And understanding made a difference. By changing her tack accordingly, my friend was able to speak his language, let him see her point of view – quite simply, get through to him.

Everyone runs different personality patterns in different contexts. So, in every new context, start from scratch and judge again.

Actions

What people do will show you who they are. So someone who has a routine for holiday packing is likely to be more procedures-oriented. Someone who likes to rethink their packing list every time they go away is likely to be driven more by options.

And what people won't do or can't do will also show you who they are. If they won't allow anyone near a project they're involved in, they're likely to be more of an independent. If they can't operate without group support, they're likely to be more of a team player.

So to spot whether someone has a particular personality pattern, get clear in your mind the general signs of action and reaction that pattern produces. Watch out for those, in what someone is doing and not doing.

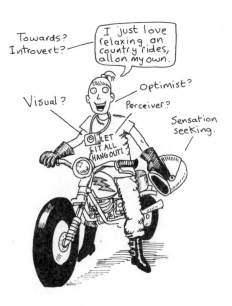

And particularly, watch when they're trying hard or just a little under stress. Because stress exaggerates personality patterns – and exaggeration makes it easier to see what's happening. Under pressure, someone who likes sameness will want to keep things extra, extra stable. Under pressure, someone externally-inspired will try to please all of the people, all the time.

Analyse people's personality patterns one by one. Choose the most vital pattern – and only move to explore another once you've really analysed the first.

Words

What people say shows you their personality just as much as what they do. So people will talk most about what's important to them. If you're listening to a towards person you'll hear a lot about goals and aims; if you're listening to an away-from person you'll hear a lot about problems and solutions.

And people will talk more positively about personality patterns they feel most comfortable with. They'll praise, congratulate and glow when faced with patterns that mirror their own. So detail-oriented people will comment that 'attention to specifics is good' while big-picture-oriented people will say that 'it's best to get the overall view'.

Conversely – of course – people will talk more negatively – or enviously – about what isn't in their personality pattern. So someone who's heavily proactive might say 'I don't understand him, he never makes the first move', or 'I really admire her, she never blunders in like I do'. Meanwhile, someone who's heavily reactive might comment 'I hate people who just rush in regardless' or 'I love folks who go for it'.

What this means is that by listening, you can often analyse people's personality very accurately. If you want to be even more accurate, ask specific questions. No need to be subtle about it – come straight out with it. 'Do you reckon you're an optimist or a pessimist?', 'what does it take to get you to believe something?' – then simply listen, very carefully, to what you hear.

Body language

What you see is very often what you get. So don't just listen to what people say – look at the way they say it.

If you hear energy in someone's voice when they're talking about beginning a project, but you hear weariness when they talk about the finishing stages, that person's probably a starter. (Reverse all that and they're probably a finisher.)

Or if you see someone's eyes defocus when bombarded with heavy specifics, but focus again when presented with a large-scale idea, that person's probably more big-picture-oriented. (Reverse all that and they're probably detail-oriented.)

Never judge someone's personality instantly. It'll take time for them to unwind and be natural, it'll take time for you to spot what's really going on.

In particular, some personality patterns have body language that beds in over time. By as young as nine and ten, some studies reckon, a person's posture and facial expression will be reflecting who they are. So an optimist – who smiles a lot – may by adulthood have pronounced smile lines and an upright posture, while a pessimist may already show frown lines and a stoop.

But a word of warning – don't get too simplistic on this. It's just not true that an extrovert's body language is always bouncy and happy (you may be seeing an introvert after three gins) or that an introvert is always quiet and withdrawn (you may be seeing an extrovert with a hangover). So ...

- don't judge from a single instance of body language, which may just be a coincidence. If someone wrinkles their nose when faced with thoughts of the future, it may mean that they are a past or present person. But it can also mean that they have an itchy nose!
- don't assume that a particular body language signal means the same thing for everyone. Not at all. Crossed arms can be a sign of blaming behaviour for some people – for others that signal will mean that they're cold, while their key blaming body language will be something completely different, such as pursed lips.
- don't look at the body language alone. Sure, it accounts for 93 per cent of what we communicate, but it's often unclear in itself and ambiguous in meaning. So, as suggested before, supplement your observation by asking questions. 'By the way, do you prefer working on your own?' 'I notice you're a bit tense – is that because you don't like the first stages of a project?' You'll get a

what makes people tick?

much more reliable result by getting the verbal as well as the nonverbal cues.

Most people don't fall on the extremes of personality patterns. So if you're confused about what personality someone has, assume that they're on the norm.

Be honest with yourself. Not everyone is motivated to spot and interpret body language. If this includes you, you may need to begin by relying on what people say and then moving on to notice what they do. And it will help to get some extra knowledge about this. The Resources section (page 293) gives some suggestions.

Trust your gut instincts. If you're unsure, don't guess someone's personality. Instead, relax, keep looking and listening and let the answer come to you.

A final tip. As you notice other people's personalities, through their actions, words and body language, it'll be very tempting to draw comparisons, make judgements, be critical. But remember that even the most irritating patterns – like constantly putting oneself down or building oneself up – have usually developed because the person needed to survive circumstances that would have turned a weaker soul into a gibbering wreck.

So although you may need to steer clear of some people, never blame them or put them down for being who they are. Instead, use this book to understand them, appreciate them, work with them.

That approach isn't just more respectful to other people. It's also more useful for you.

Using personality secrets to ... change yourself

22 When it comes to change, I'm with Benjamin Franklin. 'When you're finished changing, you're finished.' I think that it's always good to improve. So if you want to shift, then do it. Change is as possible for your personality as it is for your weight, your dress style and your hair colour.

But a word of warning. If you think you need to change your personality because there's something wrong with it, watch out. Because almost every personality pattern comes complete with a full set of built-in benefits. In fact, in my opinion, there's only one pattern in the whole of this book that has absolutely no upside at all: low self-esteem (page 35). If you have low self-esteem, that ruins everything else you do. So fix it.

But otherwise? Sure, it's a pain to be pessimistic – but studies suggest that it's also more realistic. And yes, you'll drive people up the wall if you're strong-willed – but it was strong will that got Marco Polo to China and led to the abolition of the slave trade. Even the less helpful Satir categories – blaming, placating, computing, distracting – have benefits. They may irritate other people beyond belief, but they also offer protection against conflict, defence against stress.

And when it comes to love, there's also a sneaky plus to every personality pattern. It's this: your personality is probably the absolute right one to complete the jigsaw puzzle that's your partner. He's the towards-motivated person who creates shining goals; you're the away-from person who does the downside planning to achieve those goals. Together, you have the set.

what makes people tick?

So if you want to change your personality then of course go for it. But don't throw the positive personality baby out with what you perceive to be the negative personality bath water. Instead, aim for choice. Keep the patterns you have, but get more of a spread along their spectrum. More extroversion to add to your introversion. More past to add to your future.

Change – by practising

The first step to changing your personality is deceptively simple. Decide what you want to do. Then do it.

So glance back at the sections in the main body of the book that cover personality patterns you want to develop. Many of the sections include specific hints on how to change – action plans, tip lists, things you can do in order to get the ball rolling. Read them. Do them. Take them on board.

But even the sections that don't include specific hints do include descriptions of the patterns – and you can simply decide to read those descriptions and then do what they say. In other words, play at being a someone who's highly visually biased (or a judger, or a starter, or a leveller ...).

Do it for an hour, or a day – saying, doing, thinking, feeling 'as if' you are like that.

Change – by switching contexts

I've said it a thousand times in this book – personality patterns are very contextualized. So here's the second technique.

If you can note what you're doing in one context and then do the same in another context, you'll get a shift. And it will be an easier shift because you're using talents you already have – you are working with transferable skills.

List your
personality
strengths at
work (or home)
and then map
across to home
(or work).

One friend of mine loves sameness in most areas of her life – she's stable in her relationship, loves living where she is, hangs on to her car. But in the context of clothes, she's very difference-oriented, likes one-off pieces, mix and match, her own unique style.

But she rang me in a state one day when she got stuck around decorating her lounge. She felt it was dull, but however much she tried to change it, her ideas would somehow revert again and again to identical designs and similar colours until she was bored to tears. She was working from her sameness-orientation. What could she do?

What I suggested was this. That she bring downstairs a few of her stunning outfits – heavily embroidered jackets in rich jewel colours – and hang them around the room. And then, that she start transferring her difference-oriented strategies from clothes to interior decor – in short that she realize it was OK to be a bit quirky in her living room as well as on her person.

Bullseye. Given the nudge she started to visualize how her lounge might develop a more unique style. She started to think of different textures, colours and points of interest.

The new ideas came flooding through. The lounge was re-designed, redecorated – and now looks stunningly different.

Change – by modelling

Lots of people in the world have the personality subpatterns you want. And you can have them too, by 'modelling' these people, learning from them how to be as they are.

So take time with someone more big-picture-oriented, or a future-oriented person, or a proactive soul – or, in fact, anyone who's the way you want to be. Ask them what's going on for them when they're thinking big picture, looking ahead in time, taking action.

What they say may not make sense to you at first, because – by definition – you aren't running their personality pattern. If you're detail-oriented and a big-picture-oriented thinker tells you about the broad spread of understanding she gets from her approach, you may simply not understand at first. If you love the past and a future-oriented person tries to enthuse you about their plans, you may not have a clue what he's on about.

Choose an admired celebrity, then analyse – and copy – their personality patterns.

But keep listening and learning what it is that the other person does – when, where and how. Particularly, start to appreciate what gets them fired up, what creates strong emotion. Then, as you start to understand why they do what they do, simply copy it in as much detail as you can.

Change – by advanced modelling

If you're serious about shifting your personality, then take the advanced modelling course.

Don't just copy someone else – fall in love with them. By getting very close, you soak up the other person's personality on a very deep level.

For example, when I met my high achiever, future-oriented husband I didn't have an achievement bone in my body and my idea of long-term futures was a week on Monday. Now, I love to celebrate my successes with gusto and happily plan my life a decade ahead.

Change – by getting support

Say there's a personality pattern you dislike in yourself and want to change – but you rarely spot you're running it. Your best bet is to get others in on the act. Let them help you to shift – both by pointing out when you're running the old pattern and encouraging you to run the new one.

For instance, one of my colleagues kept 'placating'. She could apologize for England, though she never realized she was doing it. Then one day, as we travelled home together from a meeting, she suddenly clocked that she'd taken all the responsibility for a corporate mess-up that wasn't anything to do with her. We had a chat about what was going on.

The arrangement we came to was this. If I spot her over-apologizing, taking the flak or running any other placator number, I use a code phrase to alert her to that. Then I'll take over the meeting for a while so that she has time to stop, think, regroup her forces and come back into the fray a little more assertively. I needed to intervene quite a lot at the start – now it's once every couple of months because she's started to take it all on board.

What I'm doing for my colleague isn't nagging. It's coaching. Personality coaching. So get as much of it as you can for yourself – and be willing to offer it, tactfully, to others when they seem to need it.

Change – by getting expert help

If the clutch went on your car, would you struggle on, driving it anyway and wrecking the internals? You would not. You would get an expert in.

So don't hold back from getting an expert in if you feel you're not achieving results in trying to shift your personality. For organizations and books that can help you with all the following suggestions, turn to page 293.

Assertiveness training

Assertiveness training has had a bad press – it's often seen as a charter to play awkward and demanding. But properly taught – and used – it helps you develop effective ways of getting what you want without alienating people.

Where can it help? It's particularly appropriate if you get influenced or follow other people's lead more than you really want to – because you're low in self-esteem (page 35), too easily convinced (believing style, page 90), overaware of others (awareness of others scale, page 137) or very externally inspired (external/internal inspiration strategy, page 151). It's also useful if conflict situations push your buttons (Satir's conflict categories, page 185).

Cognitive and Behavioural Therapy (CBT)

This support system teaches you to challenge negative thoughts as you think them and so learn to feel more positive about things.

Where can it help? It's particularly good for any personality subpatterns where you feel bad about yourself and the world, such as strong away-from motivation strategy (page 17), low self-esteem (page 35) and pessimism (page 43).

Communication skills training

Communication skills training helps you listen, talk and generally interact more effectively with other people.

Where can it help? It can help compensate for any personality subpatterns you feel limit you socially – like finding it difficult to be aware of others' experience (awareness of others scale, page 137) being too introverted (page 144) or being too independent (group interaction pattern, page 167).

Co-counselling

This is a self-help method which involves basic training in listening skills, after which you can work with someone else who's done the training, supporting each other to explore problem issues in your lives.

Where can it help? It will be most useful for tackling personality subpatterns that make you feel bad about yourself and the world, such as low self-esteem (page 35), pessimism (page 43) or being too externally-inspired (page 151).

Hypnotherapy

A hypnotherapist relaxes you completely and then works directly with your unconscious mind to change the way you think, feel and behave.

Where can it help? It's useful in changing any personality patterns, particularly if you're not sure exactly where a problem comes from and so need to work with your unconscious rather than your conscious mind.

Medication

There have been lots of interesting developments recently linking pharmaceutical intervention with general personality shifts – but currently medication is only usually prescribed if you're encountering difficulties in life. Your doctor will be able to advise you if some form of medication is suitable for you.

So where can it help? In particular, if pessimism (page 43) turns to depression or if introversion (page 144) or independence (page 167) turns to social phobia, there are medications available to help.

Neuro-linguistic Programming (NLP)

This is a relatively new type of therapy which works directly with your language and thought patterns.

Where can it help? It's relevant to all aspects of personality because it can work not only with the emotional but also the mental side of personality patterns. In particular, NLP therapy has had very good results with phobias, where what's needed is to

what makes people tick?

think differently about a traumatic incident, 'reframe' the terror around it or 'rework' one's timeline (page 62) to make the incident less harmful.

Talking therapy

Talking things through – either with an individual counsellor or in a group – helps by allowing you to explore the problem with someone else's support.

Where can it help? It's good for any personality aspects which affect you strongly, but particularly for problems with inappropriate towards/away from strategies (page 17), low self-esteem (page 35), learned helplessness (page 47) and being too externally or internally-inspired (page 151).

One branch of talking therapy is regressive therapy, where you delve back into the past in order to rethink things in the present and so sort them out. It's useful in changing any personality patterns created by early experience, like childhood abuse, bullying or trauma.

Change – even when there's a block

Personality change isn't always a breeze. Often, you hit blocks. You really try to alter your behaviour, to be more like who you want to be. But mysteriously, you fail. So why is it all going pear-shaped?

The reason may be that your particular personality is so deep-rooted, so much part of you, that subconsciously you're very wary of shifting it – particularly if you're considering shifting it to a pattern that's at opposite extremes to yours.

So you're an options person – because being anything else would feel like a straitjacket. Or you're sensation-seeking – because anything else would be dull. You're strong-willed – because anything else would make you vulnerable. You're an affiliator – because anything else would be utterly heartless. Little wonder that when it comes to it, you can't easily shift away from who you are; deep down you don't want to be anyone else.

To quickfix any personality problem, raise your self-esteem. See page 41.

The bottom line is that if you want to modify your personality, then you have to believe that the modification you're making is worthwhile. If you don't believe that, then you just won't succeed in making it.

So read back over the personality patterns as described in this book and think carefully about each one. Then look around in your life and notice who you know who runs that pattern. In particular, ask yourself whether you'd want to live the sort of life they live, with all its pros and cons.

If you do want to live that life, then now you've realized the benefits, you'll find it much easier to shift personality in that direction.

If you don't want to live that life, the answer is simple. No problem. Stay as you are and be happy.

what makes people tick?

Using personality secrets to ... understand and learn

23 Analyse your personality and you can radically improve the way you learn. And we're not just talking formal learning here – evening classes or training courses. We're talking about the learning experience of mastering a new job, adapting to a new role – even falling in love and learning the way your wonderful new partner thinks and feels.

The bottom line is this. Climb any learning curve in a way that suits your personality and you'll halve the time and effort and double the enjoyment. But climb the curve in a way that contradicts your personality and you'll get stuck halfway up, dangling by your fingertips.

Learn to suit your motivation pattern

Whatever you have to learn, make sure you're doing it for reasons which fascinate. Affiliation? Achievement? Influence? It doesn't matter – if your underlying motivation is strong, your ability to learn will be too.

See McClelland's motivator modes, page 5.

I learn Italian at evening class and have got very pally with another woman there. I – an affiliator – want to learn the language so I can talk to real Italians in restaurants, cafes, bars. She – an achiever – wants to learn because she needs the language for promotion. Same enthusiasm. Same positive end result. But utterly different motivations.

See external/internal inspiration strategy, page 151.

Use your other motivation patterns too. So if you're internally-inspired, then you won't need much push in order to learn – though if you make up your mind not to learn something, then you'll quickly blow out. And if you know you're externally-inspired, then stack the odds in favour of learning by actively enrolling people who you know will approve of what you're doing and get them to urge you along with encouragement and celebration.

And whatever you have to learn, make sure you're doing it with the right compulsion. If you're towards-motivated, set learning goals; write them down, monitor them, rejoice when you've reached them. If you're away-from motivated, you may need to remind yourself of what you're avoiding or keeping at bay by doing this learning. Ideally, of course, both set goals and avoid problems.

See towards/away from strategy, page 17.

You may wonder about this idea of using away-from motivation in order to learn – surely all learning needs to be positively motivated. But when it comes to the crunch, you'll do better to run with your personality bias – and if that involves being aware of the downside of not learning, so be it.

For example, when I started to learn Italian, I discovered that although I had a compelling vision of being able to speak it, that wasn't enough to motivate me to keep going. As a classic away-from, the thought of the goodies just didn't give me the push. Time after time I would end up on holiday having not done the work to fulfil my dream of chatting easily to the locals.

My solution? I enrolled for a course with an exam at the end of it and motivated myself just slightly by fear of failure. My husband, an inveterate towards-motivated person, got totally confused as the exam date approached. 'You're supposed to be doing this for enjoyment,' he muttered after my latest panic attack. I had to explain that giving myself a disaster to avoid was my way of making sure I worked hard.

Learn to suit your thinking pattern

Seeing, hearing, doing, reading? Which is your 'credible medium' for learning (in other words believing) something?

Much formal education specializes into auditory, word-based methods – reading, writing, listening to speech. So if you're biased towards other senses, you may not learn easily. Top up what you need with pictures, demonstrations, hands-on experience. (And remember the Chinese proverb 'I hear and I forget, I see and I remember, I do and I understand'.)

See sensory bias, page 57, and believing style, page 90.

Next, remember the repetition aspect of how you get 'to believe' (in other words, learn) something. If you need many repetitions, make sure you get them. And be aware that your need for repetition may vary. I'm 'automatic' for ideas – I pick them up almost immediately. But give me a set of facts or vocabulary to learn and I

take longer. And when it comes to physical movements, I'm 'never' – I need to memorize and memorize and even then I blank out when doing movement sequences.

See sameness/ difference strategy, page 80.

Finally, do you favour difference or sameness? If difference, give yourself lots of new ways of learning things. If sameness, then as you learn something, find parallels with what you've already learned. I made a quantum leap in my grasp of Italian when I realized just how many Italian words are very similar to English words. When I hear the word 'scissione', I can hazard a guess that it means something about cutting. In fact, it means 'split'.

Learn to suit your action pattern

When learning, think where your energy is naturally going to peak – and where it's naturally going to fade.

See starting/finishing strategy, page 103, and options/ procedures strategy, page 112.

If you're a natural starter, you'll have more energy at the beginning of the course – so make sure things get easier and more tempting later on. If you're a natural finisher, you'll be at highest energy once you've got going on the course – so make sure that the initial stages build your confidence and boost your morale.

Next, are you more options or procedures driven? For options, choose learning methods that give you choice; for procedures, choose methods that take you step by step from start to finish. In particular, choose carefully how you note-take. If you're procedures-oriented, then writing down the pages will suit you fine. But if you're options-oriented, try mindmapping, where you note every idea radiating from a central point. When it was first developed by Tony Buzan, it completely revolutionized study technique for millions of previously uninspired options-oriented students who hated the traditional procedures strategy. (Personally, as a procedures person, I've never liked mindmapping – the options diagrams make me feel confused and insecure.)

what makes people tick?

Plus, do you operate better proactively or reactively? If you're proactive, you'll want to get going, to get involved, to do – so choose active learning approaches. If you're reactive, then you'll need something to respond to – so choose classes with lots of instruction, interaction and clearly defined tasks that push you on.

See proactivity/ reactivity strategy, page 121.

Learn to suit your interaction pattern

Think about the 'people mix' you best learn with. If you're an independent or a heavy-duty introvert, you're going to be far better on your own – maybe with a distance learning course. If you're a team player or high extrovert, you'll be better with heavy interaction and lots of group activities.

See extroversion/ introversion strategy, page 144, and group interaction styles, page 167.

If you're a proximity person, then follow a course where you are in a group but largely working alone – too much individual study or too much team work will drive you spare! Or, teach the course yourself – I learned far more English literature through teaching it for seven years than I ever did during my English degree.

Learn to suit your credible source

Finally, what's your 'credible source' for education (believing style). In other words, what kind of teacher do you need in order to really learn what he or she is teaching?

See believing style, page 90.

And here you need to remember two basic truths. One: your teacher has a personality of their own. Two: their personality will always inform their teaching method. Sure, the more enlightened instructors will vary the deal so that other personality patterns get a look in. But if you find that a particular teacher is turning you off, that will be because their teaching method reflects their own personality rather than catering to yours. So either add to what they're doing with methods that suit who you are. Or find a new teacher.

A friend of mine once took two dance classes end-on every Friday, one at 6.30, one at 8.00. The teacher of the first class was an absolutely superb performer. But she was very away-from-oriented and so was her teaching style – she'd point out every tiny mistake each student made so they could correct it. Her approach wasn't wrong – lots of the class really got off on her error-spotting technique. But my friend got very demotivated.

See towards/away from strategy, page 17. The teacher of the second class, a towards-motivated person, took the approach that none of her students were ever going to dance at Covent Garden, so she didn't need to correct their errors – she simply told them when they did well. Some students objected to this because they weren't getting shown how to improve. My friend however just enjoyed the dancing.

Guess which teacher's personality patterns most meshed with my friend's patterns? And guess which class my friend carried on with the following year?

what makes people tick?

Using personality secrets to ... make the best career choice

24 Matt left school on the Thursday. On the Monday, he started work as a trainee accountant. In career terms, he was absolutely on course – his family had dreamed of this for decades, Matt had worked for this for years. He'd got the right exam results. He'd impressed at interview. His future seemed assured.

Wrong. Two years later, Matt had failed his accountancy exams, given in his notice and done the selection process for teacher training college. His family was gutted. Matt was euphoric. Now he's the head of one of the most prestigious and forward-thinking schools in Britain.

Much more importantly, he's in the right profession.

If you take a look at the personality fit, then what happened for Matt won't surprise. He's always been a team player, an options-driven thinker, someone who likes to do something different on a day-to-day level. It's an ideal personality profile for a teacher, who needs to love kids, be flexible and take whatever a day's work throws at them.

But it's the profile from hell for accountants. They don't have to be highly team-playing because their profession is often a heads-down-see-no-one-for-hours job. They do have to be procedures-driven thinkers – an accountant shouldn't be reinventing new options for double column entry book-keeping every week and accountants do need to revel in structured, controlled, repetitive tasks to get the sums right, right, right. No wonder Matt hated it.

The lesson here is pretty obvious. Whether you're choosing a

See group interaction style, page 167, options/ procedures strategy, page 112, and sameness/ difference strategy, page 80.

career from scratch or shifting midstream – as most of us will in this fast-changing world – check your personality fits. Sure, skills and qualifications are vital – you can't hack a career on personality alone, but you may have all the expertise necessary and still be both unhappy and ineffective. Matt was well *up* to being an accountant. He just wasn't *into* it.

So how can you make sure that your personality and your career have a jigsaw puzzle fit? How can you avoid finding yourself a square personality peg in a round career hole?

Profile yourself, profile your career

The list below contains 14 personality patterns that are key to career choice.

- **McClelland motivator modes - commitment to people, results, influence (page 5)**
- **Towards/away from strategy - aiming for goals or problem solving (page 17)**
- **Time strategy - being in time or through time (page 62)**
- **Time strategy - being more interested in the past, present or future (page 66)**
- **Big picture/detail strategy - preferring broad concepts or specifics (page 71)**
- **Sameness/difference strategy - preferring routine or variety (page 80)**
- **Starting/finishing strategy - preferring to begin things or complete them (page 103)**
- **Options/procedures strategy - preferring creative solutions or systems (page 112)**
- **Proactivity/reactivity strategy - taking the initiative or waiting to be sure (page 121)**

                                          what makes people tick?

- **Judging/perceiving strategy - wanting to organize life or let things flow (page 128)**
- **Awareness of others scale - understanding and empathizing (page 137)**
- **External/internal inspiration strategy - inspired by others or by self (page 151)**
- **Group interaction style - working alone, with others or in proximity (page 167)**
- **Satir conflict categories - coping or not coping with stress (page 185)**

Begin by taking an inventory of your own personality patterns. If you haven't already done so, fill out the quizzes for each pattern (page 250), then look at your scores and work out whether you are in the middle or at an extreme for each.

Now decide which are the most crucial three to six patterns, the ones you feel you most need to take into account in order to be happy in your career. These may not be the ones where you've scored on an extreme. They do need to be ones where you feel a gut sense of compulsion – where you know you're going to be seriously unfulfilled if your needs are not met.

Next, do the same profiling exercise on courses or careers you've considered. Don't try to do this off the top of your head – the more research you do, the more accurate and useful your answer will be. So read through the literature to get a sense of what the day-to-day workload entails. Get input from career specialists, who have an overview of what a particular vocational path involves. Talk to people in the field; find out what they like, what they hate. Take your time. Get lots of viewpoints, not just one.

You'll find that some personality elements simply aren't all that desirable for any chosen career – so ignore them. You'll also find that any career scores in the middle on several patterns – and high on just a few.

What you're aiming for from the information you've gathered is to identify the most important patterns – between three and six is an ideal number – the ones that characterize this career as opposed to any other, the ones that absolutely need to be there. As with your personal score, these may not be the ones where the score is extreme; they will be the ones that a person needs in order to make a success of this career direction.

Here are two examples. First, nursing. A good nurse would need to be motivated by her own values but able to follow instructions, be driven by a desire for good health and an avoidance of illness, be a team player able to work with others and be able to follow systems. So a good nurse is balanced on external/internal inspiration; balanced in towards/away from motivation; high on team; high on procedures.

LISA'S SCORES

1: McClelland motivator mode — affiliator
2: towards...away from strategy — balanced
3: time strategy — (very in time) crucial!
4: big-picture...detail strategy — fairly big picture
5: Sameness...difference strategy — balanced
6: starter...finisher strategy — (strongly starter) crucial!
7: options...procedures strategy — more options
8: proactive...reactive strategy — (strongly proactive) crucial!
9: perceiver...judger strategy — balanced
10: awareness of others scale — (very aware) crucial!
11: extrovert...introvert strategy — (very extrovert) crucial!
12: external...internal strategy — slightly more external
13: group interaction style — (very team) crucial!
14: Satir's conflict categories — leveller, with a bit of blamer

Second example – the legal profession. Lawrence Richard, an American lawyer, discovered that 63 per cent of lawyers are judgers who need to be highly organized in their work – as opposed to 55 per cent of the general population; 57 per cent of lawyers are detail-oriented people – as opposed to 30 per cent of the population; 54 per cent of lawyers also like to work alone – as opposed to 25 per cent of the general population. So a good lawyer is a high judger; high on detail; high on independence.

Is there a profile fit?

So you've profiled yourself. And you've profiled your prospective careers. The third step is pretty obvious. Is there a match?

You don't need a perfect fit. You do need to look at where your profile and the profile of your potential career vastly differ. If your career demands a heavily difference-oriented person and you're heavily sameness-oriented, there's a problem. If your career demands a balance between difference and sameness and you're heavily extreme in either subpattern, there's less of a problem, but you still need to tread carefully.

The bottom line is that if you do have a fit, then go for it. If you don't have a fit, you have three clear choices.

First, you can go for it anyway, simply grit your teeth and plough on. Sure, you may blow out, your personality rubbing against your career at every turn, but at least you've tried. And who knows – your love for your chosen profession may get you there. Some of the most famous and successful actors are – wait for it – introverts. But on stage they pull themselves together and shine. Sheer desire and willpower can overrule almost anything.

Second, you can shift your personality. Broaden your range and you may be able to find a fit – the section on changing, page 202, will help. But be very careful. Some personality patterns simply can't be shifted. Others can, but only at the expense of your sanity. Matt could have gritted his teeth and stayed an accountant – he was bright enough. But would he ever have been happy? No way.

And third, you can alter your career spec. The particular strand you've chosen is never the only one on offer – there will be other options. Say you're too much of a team player to be a librarian; so manage a book store, where you still get to be around information, but with people contact. Or say you're too independent to be a news-gathering journalist; so be a researcher where you still get to trawl for the facts, but get to work alone.

Getting stuck at the start

A warning: there are some personality subpatterns which – if you're way off-the-scale – won't help you at all at the beginning of any career path.

- **off-the-scale big-picture-oriented – you like large projects and can't be doing with the details (page 71)**
- **off-the-scale difference – you like, and are comfortable with, a great deal of change (page 80)**
- **off-the-scale starter – you love to initiate but don't have the motivation to complete or conclude (page 103)**
- **off-the-scale options-oriented: you're creative, uncomfortable with set ways of doing things (page 112)**
- **off-the-scale proactive – you love to act and never wait to be given permission to do things (page 121)**
- **off-the-scale internally-inspired – you make your own decisions without reference to external input (page 151)**

These are the creative, visionary, big-picture-type subpatterns that are magic once you've climbed the career ladder. But at the bottom

what makes people tick?

of that ladder, they'll either get you frustrated because you're not playing to your strengths – or they'll get your employers frustrated because they want the detail-oriented executive skills that are usually needed as you enter the career arena.

So if your personality has three or more of the above six patterns, then at the start of your career, people will be wary of giving you the responsibility (and the permission) to use them. You may struggle to find a cap that fits and you may stay unemployable for a while.

But as you get the responsibility and permission, then with a good following wind and the right kind of career, you'll find your niche. Your initiative, vision and big picture thinking will mean that once you've risen above the bottom rungs, you'll wing your way to the top.

Is there a way to short-circuit this process? Here are three suggestions. Take a high-grade professional qualification, which will allow you to step over the lower levels of the corporate hierarchy and go in at big-picture, policy-making level. Or join a large firm which has room for creative people at all levels of the company.

Alternatively, be born Richard Branson. He's a big-picture, difference-oriented, options-driven, proactive, internally-inspired starter – who just happens to be a multimillionaire. And no, Richard did not work his way up from the shop floor – he was a schoolboy entrepreneur, thus neatly side-stepping the classic starter trap I've just outlined. He probably realized fairly early on that with his particular blend of personality patterns, he was much better off not even attempting to fit into anyone's company as an employee.

So he started his own company and the rest is history. Nice one, Richard.

Getting stuck later on

Here's the other side of it. There are some patterns which will have you doing fabulously well at the start of your career. But if over time you don't shift them slightly, don't broaden your scope, you'll hit that glass ceiling.

- **off-the-scale detail – you like working on specifics and find it difficult to think about the big picture (page 71)**
- **off-the-scale sameness – you like stability and are uncomfortable with development and change (page 80)**
- **off-the-scale finisher – you love completing, but are uncomfortable starting projects (page 103)**
- **off-the-scale procedures-oriented – you like to work to existing systems, rather than thinking up new solutions (page 112)**
- **off-the-scale reactive – you respond to requests, but feel uncomfortable acting on your own initiative (page 121)**
- **off-the-scale externally-inspired – you're guided by others, find it hard to make your own decisions (page 151)**
- **off-the-scale independent or team – you find it uncomfortable to take the lead (page 167)**
- **off-the-scale 'my rules for me, your rules for you' or 'your rules for you, your rules for me' – you find it difficult to set standards for other people, so are not comfortable in management (page 176)**

These are the small-chunk, executive, get-things-done subpatterns that make you utterly wonderful on the lower rungs of a career ladder, that make you an ideal assistant or employee. But as you climb up that ladder and get asked to think bigger, wider, more creatively and more proactively, you'll stumble. And the danger is that, if promoted into a management or policy post, you'll be disaster on legs. Yes, you may make the promotion leap – but you'll probably hate it. Or worse, you'll get hated – and then get fired.

So if you know your personality matches more than four of the above eight patterns, you have to face facts. However much you lust after project control, people management and decision-making responsibility, such things won't be natural to you. If you want to be truly successful, you'll need to get a lot more up to speed in all the personality patterns listed here – and that will mean getting training, development and support to make your upward move.

That direction is eminently doable. But there is an alternative. Don't move. Dig your heels in and stay put. Why not? There's no failure in deciding to do the things you like and are suited for. Remaining at the 'second-in-command' or 'non-policy-making' levels of a career path may well be the best thing you can do for yourself.

It may also be the kindest thing for your employers. Because here's a cautionary tale about promotion without the appropriate personality.

In the eighties, there was launched a women's magazine. The editor was internally-inspired, proactive, very options-driven – exactly the right creative decision-maker for her post. The deputy was externally-inspired, reactive and procedures-driven – exactly the right second in command for her post. The internally-inspired editor had the vision, her deputy put that vision into action. A perfect team.

Then disaster struck. The editor moved on. Her deputy was promoted. And she was completely and utterly wrong for the job. She didn't have the focus. She wasn't able to act on her own initiative. She had no vision – and if she did manage to have a forward-thinking thought, she would then get influenced by absolutely everyone around her, including the tea lady.

She couldn't hack it. The sales figures plummeted. The magazine closed ten months later.

And the moral? When it comes to personality, either change your pattern or stick to your knitting.

Using personality secrets to ...
succeed at interview

25 Here's the bad news. There's no 'personality fix' for interviews. You can't win by pretending you're a different personality. You can't win by manipulating the interviewer's personality.

Because short term, any halfway decent interviewer will read your real personality rather than the one you want them to see and will neatly sidestep any attempt to bias them in your favour. And in any case, long-term, if you don't fit with the job, the whole thing is doomed in any case.

No, the only way to succeed at interview is the straight way. Find out, when you apply, what the company wants and the post requires. And if you can't provide the fit, then walk away.

But here's the good news. If you can provide the fit, you'll be several steps ahead of most applicants – and once in the post, you'll be both superbly successful and supremely happy.

So begin by reminding yourself of the most central patterns of your personality profile when it comes to career choice (see page 217). Then, set about profiling not only the job you're applying for, but also the company you're applying to. You need a personality fit with both – company culture as well as the demands of the specific post.

Company culture

Every company's got its own embedded personality. If you don't fit with that, you won't fit in.

what makes people tick?

I learned this one very early on. My first job was in an influence-oriented school, where teachers shouted at the children, the staff pulled rank on each other the whole time, the headmistress was power crazy and I was utterly miserable. One job change later, I ended up in a very affiliation college, where there was a lot of colleague and student support – and I blossomed.

So how can you make sure that your personality and the company's personality fit? Get your initial impression of company culture from the advert and job application pack. Most companies want to put over their self-image in these and so they're a good first step. But be careful – the image in the advert may well be just that – image not reality.

If you find that your personality patterns don't suit the promotion or career shift you're aiming for, then it's possible to broaden your personality range (see page 202).

So also ask around. Talk to people who've worked for the company and to people still there who have their ears to the ground. Plus, notice what's happening when you visit the firm and get a chance to see the situation for yourself – both as you walk through the workplace and during the interview. Discover just where the firm is at the moment – in terms of motivation, organizational style, speed of change and stress levels. And then decide whether that's where you want to be.

Basic company motivation

Does the firm have a strong affiliation-, achievement- or influence-oriented culture? In other words, do you get a sense that it's friendly and supportive, interested mainly in results or hierarchy driven?

See McClelland's motivator modes, page 5.

If the company's evenly balanced between the three, you'll almost certainly fit unless you're off-the-scale in one of these respects.

If the company's off-the-scale in one direction and you're clearly going in another, think again.

Evidence of affiliation

- The job ad and application pack mention 'people', the 'team', go into detail about the personality they want to appoint and list employee perks (because the firm is very people-oriented).
- The workplace is open-plan with lots of noisy interaction on first name terms; sports announcements on the notice board; a sense that everyone's going down to the wine bar after work.
- The interview may involve staff from all levels of the firm, because the company wants them to get involved in the decision. Or, it can be an informal chat over a few pints down the pub followed by a job offer and a handshake. (Don't laugh, it happens!)

Evidence of achievement

- The job ad and application pack mention 'getting ahead' and 'reaching your goal', go into detail on recent sales figures and contracts gained; specify bonuses and commission; list out applicant experience needed.
- In the workplace, you notice head-down work; schedule planner boards or marketing target diagrams; awards in the foyer.
- The interview is likely to be a performance-based series of tests.

Evidence of influence

- The job ad and application pack mention 'authority' and 'power', emphasize the need for market dominance; specify the 'rank' candidates will join at.
- In the workplace, you notice status symbols such as high-backed chairs; lower-ranking employees looking harried; a certain aggression in the office atmosphere.

- The interview may be held in the boardroom, with lots of hierarchy symbols to be seen and a large panel composed of people who'll be above you in the pecking order if you get the job.

In addition, watch out for motivation mixes, where not just one but two categories are what motivate a firm. Affiliation and influence – chatty and sociable, but with vicious in-fighting. Achievement and affiliation – getting a result is vital, but after the deal's done, it's everyone down the pub. Influence and achievement – a strict hierarchy tied to a sales target from hell.

Basic organizational style

How strongly judging/perceiving is the company culture? Some firms – particularly in creative professions – don't necessarily demand a high degree of organization. Other companies – particularly in professions such as accounting or the law – need everything to be sorted all the time. If you're a high-level judger or perceiver, you'll be more comfortable in a company that is also that way inclined.

See judging/ perceiving strategy, page 128.

Evidence of judging culture
- The job ad and application pack may well be standardized and highly formalized. They may mention the need for deadlines, stress super-efficient organization and ask for a high standard of work accuracy.
- In the workplace, you notice little clutter in the public spaces and on individual desks. There may be planner boards in evidence. Dress code may be formal.
- The interview will be highly structured and tightly timed.

Evidence of perceiving culture

- The job ad may stress flexibility and creativity. There may not be an application pack because the firm doesn't have the level of organization needed to produce one!
- When you visit the workplace, you get a sense that things are all over the place. Staff may work flexible hours. Dress code may be 'down'.
- The interview may be informal and unstructured, run over time and allow you to take control of the process.

Quick change?

See towards/away from strategy, page 17, sameness/ difference strategy, page 80.

Is the company committed to change? Or is it currently in change mode, expanding or contracting? If so, you need to be towards-motivated and difference-oriented; if you're not, you'll be on your knees, physically and emotionally, before a month is out.

If the company is stable or uncommitted to change, then you'll be fine unless you yourself are difference-oriented – in which case, you'll get bored within weeks.

Evidence of a high change company

- The job ad and application pack stress the future, the possibilities, the goals to be reached rather than the specific job outline – which may well be unclear to a firm in the middle of great change.
- In the workplace, you may notice a great deal of new technology – typical of high change firms – coupled with a 'fly-by-the-seat-of-your-pants' approach, because everyone is so busy coping.
- The interview could well be slightly frenetic; if you're appointed, there will be pressure to start soon because they need you!

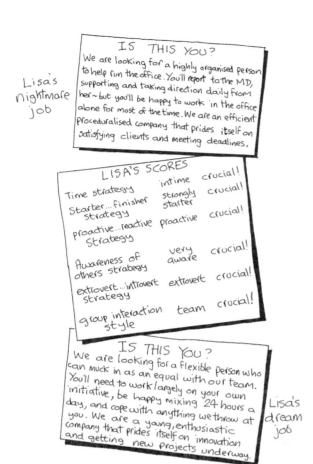

IS THIS YOU?
We are looking for a highly organised person to help run the office. You'll report to the MD, supporting and taking direction daily from her – but you'll be happy to work in the office alone for most of the time. We are an efficient proceduralised company that prides itself on satisfying clients and meeting deadlines.

Lisa's nightmare job

LISA'S SCORES

Time strategy	intime	crucial!
Starter...finisher strategy	strongly starter	crucial!
proactive...reactive strategy	proactive	crucial!
Awareness of others strategy	very aware	crucial!
extrovert...introvert strategy	extrovert	crucial!
group interaction style	team	crucial!

IS THIS YOU?
We are looking for a flexible person who can muck in as an equal with our team. You'll need to work largely on your own initiative, be happy mixing 24 hours a day, and cope with anything we throw at you. We are a young, enthusiastic company that prides itself on innovation and getting new projects underway.

Lisa's dream job

Evidence of a low change company

- The job ad and application pack mention words like 'tradition' and 'stability'. The job will be clearly defined because it's been the same for ages. The person you're replacing may well have been in post for a long time.

- When you visit the workplace, furniture, procedures or equipment may look old, but work well – they've been tried and tested over many years.

- The interview will stress the need to fit into an existing, stable situation.

High or low stress?

See towards/ away from strategy, page 17, sameness/ difference strategy, page 80, and Satir's conflict categories, page 185.

Is the company high-stress – either coping with major success or hitting crisis? If so, don't join if you're strongly towards-motivated – the problems will overwhelm you. And don't join if you lean heavily to the less helpful Satir conflict categories – you'll show your worst side and get hated.

On the other hand, is the company very low stress and low problem? If you're strongly away-from motivated, you'll quickly get bored with no difficulties to solve. And if you're very difference-oriented, then you'll quickly get frustrated because things are just the same, same, same.

Evidence of a high stress company

- The job ad and application pack mention words like 'hectic' and 'challenge', describe how busy the firm is and how flexible the appointee needs to be.
- In the workplace, you'll notice a lot of hustle and bustle, with a slightly panicky edge.
- The interview may well lack organization or even be postponed because there's yet another office crisis.

Evidence of a low stress company

- Job ads and application packs won't necessarily reflect a low stress culture.

See proactivity/ reactivity, page 121.

- In the workplace, you'll get a sense of few demands and people being relaxed. If the stress level of the firm is too low, however, you may get the sense that no one has very much to do; they're underused.
- The interview will be very relaxed.

Demands of the post

Having sussed the company personality, you then need to suss the 'personality demands' of the particular post you're applying for. Do you know what these demands are? Of course you do; you've worked in the field for years.

But actually, you may not know. The job title 'personal assistant' in one firm may mean you carry out to the letter what Her Ladyship wants on an hourly basis – so you need to be externally-inspired, seriously reactive. In another firm, 'personal assistant' means that you actually run the show because His Lordship is out of the office most of the time – so you need to be internally-inspired, seriously proactive.

And the job advertisement and application pack may not help at all – because they typically don't talk about the personality of the applicant needed – or if they do, they talk in general terms like 'hardworking, creative, loyal' rather than the specific patterns this book identifies.

Even words that seem to reflect some of the personality patterns this book covers may lead you down the garden path. For example, take the phrase 'good with people'. Does that mean that you have to value people, put them at the centre of your world and hence be an affiliator (McClelland motivator modes, page 5)? Does it simply mean that you can understand and empathize with others (awareness of others scale, page 137)? Does it mean you do what others want of you (external/internal inspiration, page 151)? Does it mean you have to be a team player, happy only when you are working with others (group interaction style, page 167)? See the problem?

So the bottom line is that you will have to do your homework here. Find out as much as you can about the reality of the job. Perhaps ring and ask a few pertinent questions. Perhaps talk to other employees. Particularly, keep your eyes and ears open during the interview itself.

Here are the key patterns to consider and the key questions to ask to identify what profile the post has. As always, when exploring these issues, you're looking for the most crucial elements, the ones you think will most define the post. Plus, you're obviously looking to find a fit with your own personality profile.

- Towards/away from strategy – goal-setting, problem solving (page 17)
  Does the firm manage by bonuses (towards) or penalties (away-from)? Get a sense of whether your manager will typically encourage you (towards) or point out your errors (away-from)?
- Time strategy – being in time or through time (page 62)
  Ask whether the job demands you keep to strict time schedules. If it does, they need a through-time person; if not, then your time style doesn't matter too much.
- Time strategy – being interested in the past, present or future (page 62)
  Ask whether the job involves checking or keeping tabs on past work, responding to here and now demands or planning ahead – to determine whether you need to be past- or future-oriented.
- Big picture/detail strategy – broad concepts or specifics (page 71)
  Ask whether the post deals largely with policy and ideas – in which case; you'll need to be more big-picture-oriented. Or with the specifics – in which case, you'll need to be more details-oriented.
- Sameness/difference strategy – preferring routine or variety (page 80)
  Ask whether schedules are followed or whether every day is different. Any mention of 'the first thing we do on Monday' means sameness.

- Starting/finishing strategy – preferring to begin or complete (page 103)

  Ask your interviewers how they got their posts – if by opportunity within the firm rather than by promotion, the firm gives space to starters. Ask if you'll be getting projects up and running – if the answer is 'no', it's a finisher post.

- Options/procedures strategy – creativity or systems (page 112)

  If the post is newly defined with no real job spec, it almost certainly has an options requirement. If it's an established post with heavy induction and documentation, then it's procedures-oriented.

- Proactivity/reactivity strategy – taking the initiative or waiting to be sure (page 121)

  Ask whether the job involves making your own decisions or mostly following instructions – the former is a proactive, the latter a reactive role.

- Judging/perceiving strategy – organizing or flowing (page 128)

  Look at how organized you are expected to be and how organized others around you are. If there's a mismatch with your own style, you may feel uncomfortable.

- Awareness of others scale – understanding and empathizing (page 137)

  Get a sense of whether the post needs a great deal of empathy with others – is there a lot of support work involved or client contact? If so, you'll need to be high on this pattern.

- External/internal strategy – inspired by others or by self (page 151)

  Ask how often you'll need to check in with your manager. If monthly/yearly, they want someone internally inspired; hourly, they want someone external. Also check the level of conflicting demands you'll have to meet; if you're externally inspired, you'll be happier with few.

- Group interaction style – independent, team, proximity (page 167)

  Ask whose responsibility things are – plus how much input you get from others. The combination of answers will tell you whether you need to be more independent, more team or more proximity.
- Satir conflict categories – coping with stress (page 185)

  You may have already discovered that the firm is under stress. But even if it isn't, find out whether the post is a stressful one by asking about deadlines, conflict or heavy client demands – and the actual working hours rather than the advertised ones. If the post is stressful, then the more of a leveller you are, the more you'll be able to handle it.

The interview

So you've done your homework – about the company and the post – and you're well prepared. That means that in the actual interview, you're able to highlight not only your skills, qualifications and experience, but also the personality patterns that make you right for the job. But how best to do this?

First, be upfront. Say clearly that you have a particular personality and that it fits with the job. 'I'm the future-oriented person that you say this role needs, I've got the finishing skills that you're asking for, I've the empathy you want, I can stay calm when doing credit control ...'

Plus, give examples of your personality and, when you do, shine. At a recent interview round I was involved in – for a post that needed someone very detail-oriented – we appointed the guy who came to life when describing how he'd sooo enjoyed setting up a filing system!

Also, exploit questions that let you emphasize your personality

what makes people tick?

strengths: 'what do you enjoy about your current job? what do you find difficult? tell me about a success, what are you looking for in a job ...?' All of these can be answered with reference to your personality to emphasize the fit between you and the post.

In addition, many traditionally 'tricky' interview questions are a lot less difficult if you respond from a personality perspective: 'why are you leaving your last position, what problems have you had with colleagues, how are you developing yourself ...?' can all be tackled by saying that you're now aware of personality issues and can cope with them better than before.

See external/internal inspiration strategy, page 151, optimism/ pessimism strategy, page 43, and Satir's conflict categories, page 185.

For example, I once interviewed a candidate who, in the practical side of the interview, seemed highly towards-motivated. The post demanded a lot of problem-solving, so that worried me. But the candidate redeemed herself in the one-to-one session by volunteering that 'I know I need to develop a greater sense of what can go wrong and I've been working on that'.

But be careful. While it's fine to give a personality explanation for problems you've hit in the past, it doesn't work as well to say 'I left my previous job because there was a personality clash.' Avoid this expression – so often it comes across as code for 'I'm hell to work with.'

Equally, interviewers are very wary of the personality subpatterns 'strong-willed, pessimistic, blamer'. So if you run any of these patterns, learn not to run them at work.

And if you can't do that, at least learn not to flaunt them at an interview!

Problems

What if you come to the conclusion during the appointments procedure that your personality may not fit the job you've applied for? Personally, I'd raise the issue and clarify it with your interviewers.

The worst that can happen is that you won't get the post because it is, in fact, the wrong one for you – and in fact, if it is the wrong one for you then actually you'd be better off out of it.

And the best that can happen is that, on talking it through, you may realize that you are suited for the job after all. Or alternatively, that it's possible for the employer to shift the goalposts slightly to create a better fit. In other words, your honesty will bring its own reward.

To illustrate that, a story. On one recent application round, I interviewed an applicant who at the end of the process said that she liked variety, people and a fair amount of responsibility – and that she now realized the 'same day after day, head down, never interact' job we were offering wasn't right for her. The application board took what she said on board and didn't appoint her to the post she'd applied for ...

They did, however, appoint her to another post they had on their books, a management role where she's both happy and a great success.

Yes, this woman made a mistake by applying for the wrong job in the first place. But she got it right by being upfront as soon as she realized her mistake, so giving the company a chance to realize her actual strengths and capitalize on them.

She's happy. They're happy. Result.

what makes people tick?

Using personality secrets to ... make love work

(26) I'll be honest. If you think you've found your perfect partner, then even if this book tells you you're wrong and your relationship's a disaster, you won't actually listen. And if you think your partner is wrong for you, then even if this book proves beyond a shadow of a doubt that they're Mr or Ms Right, it won't make things any better.

But a knowledge of personality can still help you enormously in making love work. It can help you choose the right person, the one who'll be a good partner, the one who'll fit with you. And it can help you work with that fit, even when things go a bit wrong, by tweaking your personalities or by adding in skills that will help you triumph.

Partner from hell

To begin with, some personality combinations are a total disaster in the relationships department. My advice is to avoid them like the plague. Yes, of course you might be the one to make an honest man (or woman) out of one of these people. But don't say I didn't warn you.

The Casanova

- This partner is strongly towards-motivated where sex is concerned – so will do anything and everything to get you into bed. He – it usually is a he – may also be sensation-seeking, looking for sex simply for the adrenalin rush it provides. But he also looks for difference in relationships – so once the first flush of lust is over, he gets bored and moves on.
- How do you spot that? Watch out for pushiness to get you to sleep with them, plus a track record of short-term liaisons.
- For more warning information, see towards/away from strategy (page 17), sensation-seeking scale (page 50) and sameness/difference strategy (page 80).

The dictator

- This partner wants 'influence' in the relationship. They may also be 'strong-willed', a 'blamer' and believe in 'my rules for me, my rules for you'. If you're a placator, compliant or low in self-esteem, you'll add to the problem by agreeing that it's all your fault, which is probably why your partner was attracted to you in the first place.
- How do you spot that? Watch out for a need to run your life for you, for general blaming behaviour, for 'heel digging in', if at any point you try to make suggestions or say what you want to happen.
- For more warning information, see McClelland motivator modes (page 5), external/internal inspiration strategy (page 151), group standards model (page 176), and Satir's conflict categories (page 185).

what makes people tick?

The misery guts

- This partner is a heavy duty away-from who typically starts a relationship scared of the alternative – loneliness, for example. But then, they start moving 'away from' certain things in the relationship with you. Alternatively, they're a pessimist. At the start, the sheer euphoria of being in love creates positivity. But soon, the focus is on the worst in everything – life with you or without you – which is not easy to live with.
- How do you spot that? Watch out for constant talk of 'what's gone wrong' – particularly about past relationships.
- For more warning information, see towards/away from strategy (page 17) and optimism/pessimism strategy (page 43).

The self-obsessed

- This partner is unaware of others – so hooked up in their own head that they can't even begin to empathize with what you're feeling. Plus they make it impossible for you to get close or bond.
- How do you spot that? Watch out for someone who doesn't actually register what you're doing or feeling. In bed, you get a choreographed routine rather than a genuine response to what's happening with you, right here, right now. And if you ask for support or help, there's always a reason why you shouldn't be asking or they shouldn't be responding.
- For more warning information, see awareness of others scale (page 137).

Partner from heaven

Thank heavens, to balance out the disasters, there's a set of personality combinations that naturally make for loving partners. Quite simply, people like this are more likely to come up with the goods in the relationship department. So when you're sorting out the sheep from the goats in the dating game, keep an eye out for them.

The equal partner
- This is someone balanced between taking their own and other's needs into account. If they can balance the two, they'll be more likely to offer you an equal relationship rather than a dependent or dominant one.
- How do you test for that? When your partner has a decision to make, watch how they make it. If they actively ask for advice but finally make up their own mind – rather than relying completely on other people's views, or refusing to listen to input from anyone else – then they have a balanced strategy.
- For more information, see external/internal inspiration strategy (page 137).

The fair fighter
- This is someone who 'levels' – argues cleanly rather than 'placating', 'blaming', 'distracting' or 'computing'. Someone who goes for win-win solutions all the time will be able to overcome the conflicts that every couple has.
- How do you test for that? Ask your partner about the last disagreement he or she had with someone. The more they report that things were sorted in a win-win way – rather than taking the blame, dishing out the blame, wandering into irrelevancies

or cutting off into logic – the more of a 'leveller' they are.

- For more information, see Satir's conflict categories (page 185).

The secure in himself

- This is someone who has high self-esteem. It's very good news – a person who feels good about themselves will have more love to spare for you.
- How do you spot that? When faced with success or failure in their lives, they neither put themselves down, nor boost themselves up – they seem at ease with themselves and have genuine attention to give to others.
- For more information, see self-esteem scale (page 35).

The sympathizer

- This is the direct opposite of the self-obsessed partner from hell – someone who can 'step into' how you are feeling. Their high-level awareness skills means that they have the potential to understand you deeply.
- How do you test for that? After you've been somewhere together, start a conversation about the people you met. The more your partner shows interest and insight into what others were doing and feeling – rather than seeming confused or disinterested – the more aware they are.
- For more information, see awareness of others strategy (page 137).

Getting the fit

Choosing the right partner isn't just a case of avoiding the disasters and heading for the goodies. You also choose for complementarity.

And here, the 'opposites attract' rule isn't just a neat saying. Opposites do attract, because they complement. So if you're an introvert, then the fabled glance across a crowded room may well find you an extrovert who you just know is going to brighten your life with their social competence. In the meantime, their subconscious is clocking that your calm, cool introvert exterior is just what they need to give them some peace and quiet. Click.

Actually, you may know this already. If you've ever fallen in love, you'll have already had an experience of feeling that another person is more insightful, more loving, more creative than you are. In fact, what that means is that this other person doesn't have your personality patterns – and those they do have seem wonderful because they're different.

In fact, when you choose a partner, something interesting often happens. For the two or three patterns in your personality that are at an extreme, you'll often get drawn – without realizing it – to someone with those patterns at the opposite extreme, to balance out your jigsaw pieces with theirs.

And this is a good thing – because of the complementarity issue. Your off-the-scaleness in one respect both complements and is complemented by, your partner's off-the-scaleness in the opposite respect.

So go with that. It'll work, giving you a balance of personality elements, making the two of you together more effective in the world than one of you on their own.

Five very useful partner fits – catch them if you can!

- *Towards/away from strategy* One of you heads only for what attracts you. The other is motivated by avoiding trouble. You click – and make an effective couple – because you love each other's enthusiasm or problem-solving ability (towards/away from strategy, page 17).
- *Big picture/detail strategy* One of you likes ideas and big-picture

stuff. The other likes the small bits of life. You click because you love each other's vision or eye for specifics (big picture/detail strategy, page 71).

- *Sameness/difference strategy* One of you likes stability. The other loves change. You click because you love each other's reliability and consistency or sense of novelty (sameness/difference strategy, page 80).
- *Starting/finishing strategy* One of you loves getting things going. The other loves finishing things. You click because you love each other's energy for starting or getting things done (starting/finishing strategy, page 103).
- *Judging/perceiving strategy* One of you enjoys life drifting by. The other loves having things sorted and settled. You click because you love each other's easy-going nature or organized approach to life (judging/perceiving strategy, page 128).

For example, you're a starter, he's a finisher – so he or she can get things going while you make them happen. You're a towards-motivated person, he's an away-from – so she or he can check for problems while you're concentrating on vision.

At some level, often subconscious, your personalities realize they've met their match. Click. Double click. Fit. Perfect fit.

Losing the fit

But – and it's a big but – however good a fit your initial click, a while down the line, it may well start to wear thin. That's because these personality fits depend on difference. This complementarity depends on not being identical. And in the end, this lack of similarity is going to irritate you – or worse.

Here are how partner personality fits go wrong

- *Towards/away from strategy* You originally clicked because you loved each other's enthusiasm or problem-solving ability. But after a while, the towards partner gets bugged by constantly being told about the problems; the away-from partner tires of unbounded and relentless positivity.
- *Big picture/detail strategy* You originally clicked because you loved each other's vision or eye for specifics. But now the big-picture partner gets bored hearing every last little daily detail whilst the detail partner fazes out at ideas, ideas, ideas.
- *Sameness/difference strategy* You originally clicked because you loved each other's reliability or sense of novelty. But now the sameness partner feels constantly pushed to move house, move job, change car, whilst the difference partner feels trapped by every day feeling the same.
- *Starting/finishing strategy* You originally clicked because you loved each other's energy for new projects or ability to get things completed. But now the starter partner feels boxed in by having to complete things they've lost interest in whilst the finisher gets resentful because nothing's ever done.
- *Judging/perceiving strategy* You originally clicked because you loved each other's easy going nature or organized approach to life. But now the judger feels totally disorganized whilst the perceiver feels continuously hassled.

The bad news is that if you carry on feeling negative about personality differences like these and let them turn into the basis for daily rows, then, to be blunt, your relationship is doomed.

Glorious futures

The good news is that if you can hang in there, then in time you can reverse the negativity. Because the personality differences start to become a strength rather than a liability.

The bottom line is that, if you can learn to live with a partner who isn't exactly the same as you, then you'll have a better and more workable relationship than partners who are the same and don't fill in each other's gaps. So how to get to this point? How to feel as good about your partner's personality patterns as you do about your own?

Here are six suggestions for regaining your personality fit

- Take it on the chin. Don't deny that there are differences — instead accept and value them.
- Talk about the differences. Really understand how the other operates. Ask how and why. Get fascinated by the difference, not fazed.
- Read through the sections in this book which cover the personality patterns where you differ. Learn about each other, particularly why you are the way you are. Many of these sections also offer in-depth advice on how to bridge the gap and resolve your differences.
- Pick up some patterns from each other, learning how to do the bits that the other one can do so well. You'll gradually become closer, more similar in some ways.
- Alternatively, specialize into your roles. Let your partner do their thing — don't expect them to do your thing. If you can both do that, you'll not only each be doing what you're best at. More, you'll each be compensating for the other's gaps and weaknesses.
- When each of you has done your individual thing, to the best of your ability, thank each other nicely and be grateful.

My husband and I are a case in point. When we met, we were both totally inspired by each other. I loved hearing him dream. He, meanwhile, was in awe of my ability to organize; he loved the way I had my life in order.

He, in case you need a more specific analysis, was at the time a heavily future-oriented, options-driven, reactive perceiver. I was a present- and past-oriented, procedures-driven, proactive judger.

But as time went on, I realized that I was the one who had to make things happen. So what was he doing? Just dreaming. I got resentful.

In the meantime, he was busy getting fratchy at my seeming need for over-organization. Why did I always want action here and now? Why was I always trying to get things sorted?

There followed a long period of head to head. But after a while, we not only got over the arguments and started to understand each other, in time, he also learned from me how to make things happen and I learned from him how to see off into the future. And we also slowly realized what we'd actually known from the start – that we really needed each other's very different approaches to life.

The plans my husband was making were ones I never would have dreamt of – a superbly eccentric house, creative and inspirational work projects, a series of weird and wonderful holidays. The organization I was doing was stuff that he'd never have ever realized had to be done – the fine details of the mortgage, the organization to make the work happen, the scheduling of the itineraries. Without him, I wouldn't have ever dreamed of any of it. Without me, he wouldn't have been able to bring the dreams into reality. We'd both appreciated these characteristics in each other when we'd fallen in love. We just had to start re-appreciating all over again.

Now? Now he has the initial ideas. I do the practicalities. And then we both knuckle down – in our very different ways – to make things happen.

Towards big picture,
Difference,
Starter,
Perceiver,
Extrovert. →

← Away from detail,
Sameness,
Finisher,
Judger,
Introvert.

This story is, in fact, only a reflection of the crucial point which I made at the very beginning of this book, which is as follows.

Every personality is unique. There will never be anyone else in the world with the same personality as you. Everyone has a mix of different traits, in different amounts, with a different balance.

If you can accept that, appreciate it and build on it, then you will be a long, long way down the road to being successful, effective ... and happy.

Quiz guidelines

These quizzes will enable you to discover your personality. Here are some guidelines to help you get the most out of them.

Answering the quiz

- Do each quiz before reading the relevant section in the book. Otherwise you may find yourself answering the quiz in a way that gives you the personality you want!
- If any question doesn't apply to your life at the moment, imagine there's an 'if' at the beginning of the question and answer it 'as if' you were in that situation.
- If you find it hard to choose between quiz answers, that probably means that you aren't clearly at one extreme or the other on that personality pattern. Choose the answer nearest your situation.

Scoring the quiz

- In general, the higher you score on any subpattern, the more that will influence your personality. If the quiz results in a number of scores for different components, then the highest scoring component influences your personality most. For example, in the first quiz – basic fascinations – there are three lists so you will have three scores. Your highest score is the element that influences your personality most.
- If two or more components within a quiz score equally highly, they'll all influence your personality, perhaps driving you

equally, perhaps pulling you in different directions. When you read the relevant section of the book, bear that possibility in mind.

- If you find yourself scoring at one extreme on some questions or components in a quiz and at the other extreme on other questions or components, then you may be running that particular personality pattern differently in different contexts, at different times or with different people.
- Scoring low on one aspect of a pattern is as interesting as a high score. It may be a wake-up call – you need to boost that component of your personality. It may also be a mine detector for prejudice – because most of us are either envious or wary of the elements we don't have.

Once you've done the quiz, read the section in the book that's relevant to the quiz you've completed. After that, it's useful to go back and look again at your quiz answers, in the light of what you now know about that personality pattern and how it applies to you.

Quizzes

Quiz: basic fascinations

Here are three lists – A, B and C. For each statement score: 0 if it is nothing like you, 1 if it is sometimes like you, 2 if it is exactly like you. Then add up your total for each list.

List A

	score 0, 1, or 2

- I try hard to regularly keep up with friends and family. _____
- I love sitting in public places, people watching. _____
- I find human nature endlessly fascinating. _____
- I admire voluntary workers; they give up so much to help others. _____
- I couldn't respect a partner who trampled on others' feelings. _____
- I wouldn't take a promotion if I felt it would affect my relationship. _____
- When I die, I'd like to know that people close to me mourned me. _____

Add up the numbers to find your total for list A   TOTAL = _____

List B

- I get a buzz out of doing things better than others do. _____
- If I think I'm going to fail at something, I just lose interest. _____
- I thrive on working in a competitive environment. _____
- I give myself pep talks to make myself do better. _____

what makes people tick?

- I notice and aspire to people who are successful in their own fields.   _____
- I find it a real buzz if a partner shines in some aspect of their life.   _____
- It's important for me to feel that I'm always improving myself.   _____

Add up the numbers to find your total for list B   TOTAL =   _____

List C

- I like to bring people round to my way of thinking.   _____
- I'd like to be remembered for the influence I had on people's lives.   _____
- Sometimes I deliberately disagree with people, to get a response.   _____
- I get a buzz from being in charge.   _____
- At a social/work gathering, I like everyone to feel my presence.   _____
- In a pride of lions, I'd like to be the dominant male/female.   _____
- I respect powerful people and aspire to be like them.   _____

Add up the numbers to find your total for list C   TOTAL =   _____

How did you score?

This quiz tests what fascinates you, motivates you, gives purpose to your life. There are three patterns here. Your score on list A shows how much you're motivated by *affiliation* – that is, people. Your score on list B shows how much you're motivated by *achievement* – that is, success. Your score on list C shows how much you're motivated by *influence* – that is, being in charge.

You can find a full exploration of this personality pattern on page 5.

Quiz: carrot or stick?

Circle which statement – a, b or c – you agree with most. (Circle the actual letter not the box.)

1. I left my last job because ...
- ☐ a) I wasn't enjoying it any more.
- ☐ b) there was something better on the horizon.
- ☐ c) it was getting me down and I wanted a positive change of direction.

2. When I was at school, I studied because ...
- ☐ a) I was worried about failing.
- ☐ b) I enjoyed the feeling of doing well.
- ☐ c) of a mixture of a and b.

3. My most usual reason for taking a holiday is because ...
- ☐ a) I need a break from the 9 to 5 treadmill.
- ☐ b) I am interested in visiting a particular place and have planned to go there for a while.
- ☐ c) I need a holiday, and I find somewhere to go that I've always wanted to visit.

4. A large pay rise would be welcome to me because ...
- ☐ a) I would avoid debt; it would help keep the bills at bay.
- ☐ b) I would feel personal satisfaction, feel that I was advancing my career.
- ☐ c) of a mixture of a and b.

5. I would be more likely to end a relationship if ...
- ☐ a) I was dissatisfied and felt it was dragging me down.
- ☐ b) thoughts of freedom and being single were more exciting.
- ☐ c) it had become stale and I thought I'd feel happier alone.

what makes people tick?

6. At work I am more motivated by ...

☐ a) deadlines and pressure from my manager.

☐ b) bonuses, reaching targets and a pat on the back.

☐ c) a mixture of a and b.

7. In general, I ...

☐ a) wait until I start to feel stressed before I make changes for the better.

☐ b) continually make changes for the better in order to live life according to my aims.

☐ c) try to make changes regularly – though stress often motivates me to change.

8. In my opinion, it's better to be ...

☐ a) wary; then I can have more control.

☐ b) trusting; then I can create more opportunities.

☐ c) a mixture of a and b.

Using the boxes, fill in your scores for each question. If you circled a) score 2; if you circled b) score 2; if you scored c) score 1 point each in the a) and b) boxes.

How did you score?

This quiz looks at how you motivate yourself day-to-day – whether you're most driven 'away from' the problems or mistakes you want to avoid or 'towards' the rewards you see ahead. The quiz is based on a bipolar scale, with 'towards' at one end, and 'away from' at the other. The more marks you score for a) statements, the more away-from-motivated you are. The more marks you score for b) statements, the more towards-motivated you are.

You can find a full exploration of this personality pattern on page 17.

Quiz: being who you are

Read the following statements and circle: 3 if you strongly disagree, 2 if you disagree, 1 if you agree, 0 if you strongly agree. Then add up your total score.

	strongly disagree	disagree	agree	strongly agree

Work

• If my boss ticked me off for making a mistake, I would feel very annoyed with myself for letting people down.	3	2	1	0
• If I had to introduce myself to a group of strangers at a work function, I would feel self-conscious.	3	2	1	0
• I would feel uncomfortable asking my boss for a pay rise.	3	2	1	0
• I would probably make a fool of myself if I had to give a presentation with no preparation.	3	2	1	0
• At work, I would keep quiet even if I disagreed with a new procedure.	3	2	1	0

Now add up your total _____

Relationships

• If my relationship had been rocky for several months, I would still stick with it – in case I didn't find anyone better.	3	2	1	0
• I'd lack the confidence to ask a gorgeous man/woman if I could buy him/her a drink.	3	2	1	0

what makes people tick?

	strongly disagree	disagree	agree	strongly agree
• If my partner had an affair and we were in a committed relationship, I would feel responsible in some way.	3	2	1	0
• After a first date, I would usually wait for the other person to phone me and suggest meeting up again.	3	2	1	0
• If I saw my partner checking out another member of the opposite sex, I'd tend to believe that I wasn't good enough for them.	3	2	1	0

Now add up your total _____

Social activities

	strongly disagree	disagree	agree	strongly agree
• If I was having a meal in the non-smoking part of a restaurant and a woman lit a cigarette, I'd wait for a waiter to point it out rather than do so myself.	3	2	1	0
• If my credit card was refused when I had a big queue of people behind me in a shop, I would feel embarrassed and give myself a hard time.	3	2	1	0
• If I had to attend a party where I hardly knew anyone, I would feel very uncomfortable and unsure of myself.	3	2	1	0
• I wouldn't complain about poor service to an unsympathetic shop assistant because it would be too awkward.	3	2	1	0

	strongly disagree	disagree	agree	strongly agree
• If my neighbour's fence kept blowing down into my garden, I would put it back up myself as I wouldn't want to make a fuss.	3	2	1	0

Now add up your total _____

Now add up your total for all three sections _____

How did you score?

This quiz tests your self-esteem. Your potential score is between 0 and 45 – the higher your score, the more belief you have in yourself. The individual sections give you additional subtotals for different areas of your life – work, relationships and social activities; you can then see how high your self-esteem is in different contexts.

It's interesting to note that when we tested this quiz as part of the preparation for the book, the scores varied enormously – from 10 to 34 – with most people scoring in the twenties range.

You can find a full exploration of this personality pattern on page 35.

Quiz: sunshine or showers

Here are two lists – A and B. For each statement score: 0 if it is nothing like you, 1 if it is sometimes like you, 2 if it is exactly like you. Then add up your total for each list.

List A

- I believe bad things happen for a reason and they often make you a better person. _____

- If I had a lot of debt, I'd think positively and concentrate on paying it off. _____

- When I start a new job, I'm hopeful that it will turn out well. _____

- If I think about getting a pet, I mainly think of the hours of fun and joy it'd bring rather than the hard work involved. _____

- If I'd been seeing less of my partner, I'd make the best of the time we did spend together. _____

- If my new house needed a lot of work, I'd look forward to the finished result. _____

List B

- If a partner of mine kept getting home late, it would probably cross my mind that they were up to something. _____

- When I worry about a situation, planning what I'll do in the 'worst-case scenario' helps me get through it. _____

- When my day starts off badly, I believe it will carry on like that or get worse. _____

- Going on holiday is great, but I do get post-holiday blues. _____

- I never plan too far into the future because you never know what will happen. _____

List A

- I can see something special in almost everyone. _____

- If I'd been unlucky in love, I'd still believe there was a special someone out there for me. _____

- If I lost my job, it would be an opportunity for me to start afresh. _____

TOTAL _____

List B

- In the past, I've been wary of getting involved with someone because relationships can so easily go wrong. _____

- Sometimes I think someone out there in the great beyond is enjoying trying to make my life difficult for me. _____

- I've usually got something on my mind, no matter how small. _____

- In life I feel it's important to be realistic and be prepared for all outcomes. _____

TOTAL _____

How did you score?

This quiz looks at what you notice most in life, the positives or the negatives – whether you are an optimist or a pessimist. The quiz is based on a bipolar scale, with 'optimist' at one end, and 'pessimist' at the other. The more marks you score on list A, the more optimistic you are. The more marks you score on list B, the more pessimistic you are. You can find a full exploration of this personality pattern on page 43.

what makes people tick?

Quiz: how high can you go?

Circle which statement, a or b, you agree with most (circle the letter not the box).

1. People into extreme sports ...
- ☐ a) must have a death wish.
- ☐ b) must have a great time; I love trying different, risky sports.

2. When I think of doing something risky, my first thought is ...
- ☐ a) it's worth doing it for the high afterwards.
- ☐ b) what's the point in putting myself in unnecessary danger?

3. My aim while on this planet is to ...
- ☐ a) find peace of mind and security.
- ☐ b) experience life to the full.

4. Would I do a parachute jump?
- ☐ a) Definitely.
- ☐ b) No way.

5. I prefer life to be ...
- ☐ a) stable and calm.
- ☐ b) full of novelty; otherwise I can get easily bored.

6. In my love relationships ...
- ☐ a) I quickly get bored and like to move on.
- ☐ b) I like stability and tend to stay with the same partner.

7. When it comes to smoking, drinking and taking recreational drugs I ...
- ☐ a) do two or all three regularly.
- ☐ b) do one or none.

8. If I saw an advert asking for volunteers to test a new medical drug, I would ...

☐ a) turn the page; it doesn't interest me.

☐ b) apply; it could be an interesting experience.

Work out your score like this: Q1 a=0 b=1; Q2 a=1 b=0; Q3 a=0 b=1; Q4 a=1 b=0; Q5 a=0 b=1; Q6 a=1 b=0; Q7 a=1 b=0; Q8 a=0 b=1 _____ = TOTAL SCORE

How did you score?

This quiz tests how high you rate on a sensation-seeking scale – your need for life stimulation. Your potential score is between 0 and 8 and the higher your score, the more of a sensation seeker you are.

Remember as you look at your scores that there are many different sorts of stimulation on offer in life – and the quiz doesn't differentiate between those. So when you're reading the full exploration of the sensation-seeking scale (on page 50), start to become aware which sorts of sensation you actively want and which you're positively wary of.

Quiz: a sense of importance

For each statement tick which one sense – visual (sight), auditory (hearing), or kinaesthetic (feeling) – would be most important to you in each given context. Then add up how many statements you ticked in each of the columns.

	VISUAL	AUDITORY	KINAESTHETIC
1. You would prefer to catch up with a friend by …	☐ email	☐ a phone call	
2 You've got space for one item when packing to go away. Which is more likely to be the 'must have' item?		☐ a personal stereo	☐ comfy shoes
3. The most important criterion when buying an item of clothing is …	☐ how it looks on		☐ a comfortable fit and the general feel
4. During lovemaking, the most sensual thing for you is …	☐ seeing your partner naked	☐ hearing your partner talking softly	☐ feeling your partner's skin
5. Which would be the most frustrating to wear all day?	☐ a blindfold	☐ earplugs	☐ padded gloves
6. The most important criterion when buying a computer keyboard would be that …	☐ the design looks stylish	☐ the keys make a satisfying sound	☐ it's comfortable to use
TOTALS	_____	_____	_____

How did you score?

This quiz looks at the order of importance that the three main senses – visual, auditory, and kinaesthetic – have for you. Your score under the visual column shows how much you value what you *see*. Your score under the auditory column shows how much you value what you *hear*. Your score on the kinaesthetic column shows how much you value what you *feel*.

You can find a full exploration of this personality pattern on page 57.

Quiz: woods or trees

Take a look at the picture below. Write down what you first notice about it.

This quiz looks at your approach when you're taking in information. Do you look first at the 'big picture' and then notice the detail? Or do you first register the detail and from that, build up the big picture? Your first reaction to the illustration will show you your intuitive style.

If you first noticed simply that it's a bar scene or there's a bunch of people in a pub – or a general overview – then you are more concerned with the big picture first.

If you first noticed the woman playing darts, that it's quiz night, the dog, the man on the phone, the football fan, the barman's picked nose – or any other specifics – then you are more concerned with detail first.

Remember that it's highly likely you will notice both sets of information – the issue is which grabs your attention first.

You can find a full exploration of this personality pattern on page 71.

what makes people tick?

Quiz: equilibrium or metamorphosis?

Read the following statements and circle: 3 if you strongly disagree, 2 if you disagree, 1 if you agree, 0 if you strongly agree. Then add up your total score.

	strongly disagree	disagree	agree	strongly agree
• I value stability and like my world to be familiar.	3	2	1	0
• I dislike change – I find it unsettling.	3	2	1	0
• I can see myself staying in the same house for several years to come.	3	2	1	0
• I can see myself staying with the same company for several years to come.	3	2	1	0
• I like to go on holiday to the same place every year.	3	2	1	0
• I probably wouldn't notice if a painting wasn't straight in an art gallery.	3	2	1	0
• I like to eat at the same pub/restaurant.	3	2	1	0
• I like my job because it's the same day-to-day and so I feel in control.	3	2	1	0
• I wouldn't notice if my boss had their hair cut.	3	2	1	0
• If my partner wanted me to move with him or her to another part of the country, I would be wary of the change.	3	2	1	0

Now add up your total   TOTAL _____

How did you score?

This quiz looks at whether you feel most comfortable when things are the same or different. The quiz is based on a bipolar scale, with 'sameness' at one end, and 'difference' at the other.

If you were to score exactly 15, then you'd be on the mid-line, precisely balanced between the two extremes. The further below 15 you are, down to 0, the more you notice and prefer sameness. The further above 15 you are, up to 30, the more you notice and prefer difference.

You can find a full exploration of this personality pattern on page 80.

Quiz: trust but verify

This quiz tests a personality pattern which has three subsections. Hence it has three quizzes. For each question place a, b, c and d in order of importance to you, by giving the most important a score of 4, the next most important a score of 3, the next most important a score of 1 and the least important a score of 0.

Set 1 – How do you need to get the proof?

1. The latest digital camera is on the market; what would convince you to choose it?

a) Reading a review in a magazine. Score ...

b) Being told by someone that it's a good buy. Score ...

c) Demonstration of how the camera worked. Score ...

d) Trying out some different cameras. Score ...

2. What would persuade you that a new destination was a good place to go on holiday?

a) Reading a recommended guide on it. Score ...

b) Chatting with someone who'd been and said it was beautiful. Score ...

c) Seeing pictures in a brochure. Score ...

d) Trying it out but – because I wouldn't know for certain until I'd been. Score ...

3. **What would be most important in persuading you to buy a particular washing machine?**

   a) Reading a consumer report comparing various new washing machines. Score …

   b) Overhearing a couple saying how pleased they were with it. Score …

   c) The look of the washing machine alongside my other kitchen appliances. Score …

   d) Using the particular washing machine before. Score …

4. **Imagine you have just won a fortune. You have been approached to invest the money in an up-market coffee bar franchise. What would convince you to commit?**

   a) Reading a favourable article on the venture in a reputable financial or trade magazine. Score …

   b) Someone already involved in the venture telling me of its success. Score …

   c) Going to a presentation on the company. Score …

   d) Checking out another one of the franchises to see how it works in practice. Score …

5. **Your child is due to start school. How could you be convinced that the local school is good enough?**

   a) Reading the latest official School Inspectors report. Score …

   b) Talking to other parents whose kids go there. Score …

   c) Seeing impressive figures on pupil's exam results. Score …

   d) Going along to the open day. Score …

Now copy down your scores into the following grid and add them up.

	Option a)	Option b)	Option c)	Option d)
Question 1				
Question 2				
Question 3				
Question 4				
Question 5				
TOTAL				

How did you score?

Your score on set 1 shows your credible medium – how the proof of something needs to be presented in order for you to be convinced. If your top score is in column a, you prefer *written evidence*. If your top score is in column b, you prefer *verbal evidence*. If your top score is in column c, you prefer *visual evidence*. If your top score is in column d, you prefer *hands-on evidence*.

Set 2 – Who needs to give you the proof?

1. How do you know whether or not to see the latest blockbuster film?

   a) I'm not interested in other people's opinion, if I fancy it, I'll see it. Score ...

   b) I'll go if the box office viewing figures are good. Score ...

   c) My friends enjoyed it and we usually like the same things. Score ...

   d) A well-known film expert said it was worth seeing. Score ...

2. You've got painful sinuses, probably infected. Who would convince you to take antibiotics?

   a) Myself, if I believed I needed them. Score ...

   b) I checked it out on the Internet. Score ...

   c) Someone close to me. Score ...

   d) My doctor. Score ...

what makes people tick?

3. We're told 5–8 pieces of fruit and veg per day are good for us. But who or what could convince you?

a) I'm only convinced if I believe it makes sense to me. Score …

b) Reading scientific proof that people who eat plenty of fruit and veg have fewer illnesses. Score …

c) If a friend/family member gave me the advice – I trust them. Score …

d) Experts – after all they know their stuff. Score …

4. A new, pricey restaurant has opened in your neighbourhood. You would be most likely to try it if …

a) you thought it looked worth the money. Score …

b) it had a recognized award for good food/service. Score …

c) friends tried it and enjoyed it. Score …

d) a well-known food critic raved about it. Score …

5. There's a great coat in the shops, but it's a daring choice. You'd be more convinced to buy it if …

a) you yourself thought it looked good and you felt stylish. Score …

b) you'd seen it recommended in a magazine as a 'star-buy'. Score …

c) your friend or partner liked it. Score …

d) the shop manager said they were selling like hot cakes. Score …

Now copy down your scores into this grid and total them.

	Option a)	Option b)	Option c)	Option d)
Question 1				
Question 2				
Question 3				
Question 4				
Question 5				
TOTAL				

How did you score?

Your score on set 2 shows your credible source. This tests who needs to provide the proof of something in order for you to be convinced. If your top score is in column a, your preference is *your own judgement*. If your top score is in column b, your preference is *objective proof*. If your top score is in column c, you preference is *a trusted 'friend'*. If your top score is in column d, you preference is *a credible role model*.

Set 3 – How many times do you need to repeat the proof?

1. How long does it take before you trust a new person to do a proper job at work?

a) If they consistently perform well a number of times. Score ...

b) I'd never trust anyone to do a job properly unless I checked them for a long time. Score ...

c) I can tell from the start whether or not they'll work out. Score ...

2. Your partner wants to redecorate drastically; how could they persuade you it was worth the money?

a) I'd have to discuss it with him/her a number of times in order to agree. Score ...

b) I'd really need time to think it through as it takes a lot to persuade me. Score ...

c) I'd agree straightaway if their reasons made sense. Score ...

3. What would convince you that the latest health trend (such as Pilates) was good for you?

a) If, after several classes, I felt it was doing me good. Score ...

b) I'm never sure about these new ideas; I'd need serious convincing. Score ...

c) I'd know immediately if it would be good for me. Score ...

4. A salesperson for a reputable breakdown company approaches you, claiming to be able to save you money if you swap your breakdown cover; would you swap?

what makes people tick?

a) Not at first, I'd have to be approached a number of times before I'd sign anything. Score ...

b) Probably not, I'm hardly ever convinced without proof. Score ...

c) Yes I'd sign straightaway if they could show I would save money. Score ...

5. How often do you need to see/hear an advert before you buy into it?

a) Several times. Score ...

b) Many times over a long period. Score ...

c) Only once. Score ...

Now copy down your scores into this grid and total them.

	Option a)	Option b)	Option c)
Question 1			
Question 2			
Question 3			
Question 4			
Question 5			
TOTAL			

How did you score?

Your score on set 3 shows your repetition need – how many times the proof of something needs to be repeated for you to be convinced. If your top score is in column a, you need *repetition* to believe something. If your top score is in column b, you're *almost never* convinced. If your top score is in column c, you accept something *automatically*.

In each of the three sets of questions in this quiz, you may have scored highly on just one element; this suggests that in general you're only convinced by this one element. But if you've scored more or less equally on two or even three, this suggests you've more than one way of being convinced, which either drive you equally or pull you in different directions.

You can find a full exploration of this personality pattern on page 90.

Quiz: setting the wheels in motion

Tick which statement – a or b – you agree with most.

1. At work, I get a buzz from ...

- ☐ a) instigating new ideas and projects.
- ☐ b) tying up all the loose ends of a project and completing it.

2. When it comes to home decorating I love ...

- ☐ a) coming up with new ideas though once it's all underway I can lose interest.
- ☐ b) the satisfaction of redecorating a room and seeing the final result.

3. If my friends and I decided to go on a group holiday, I'm more likely to be the one who ...

- ☐ a) has the initial thought and gets everyone interested.
- ☐ b) makes sure everyone's paid, had the right vaccinations, got their passports.

4. If I had to leave an enjoyable evening course unfinished because of other commitments, I would ...

- ☐ a) not be that bothered – I can always finish it another time.
- ☐ b) find it very frustrating – I dislike leaving things half done.

5. When I've bought a new book, I usually ...

- ☐ a) start the new one – even if I haven't finished the last one I was reading.
- ☐ b) finish the last one I was reading before starting the new one.

6. If a new relationship ended because the other person just stopped phoning, I'd be more likely to ...

- ☐ a) not be that interested in why they stopped phoning.
- ☐ b) need to find out why they had stopped phoning.

7. If a child I knew asked for help with a piece of homework, I would ...

- ☐ a) be happy to get them going but leave them to their own devices thereafter.
- ☐ b) follow up after helping them, by asking how they got on with it.

what makes people tick?

8. If a friend was halfway through telling an anecdote, but we were interrupted, I'd be more likely to ...

☐ a) forget about it as other things would claim my attention.

☐ b) need to know the end of the story and ask the friend to finish the tale at the next opportunity.

a) TOTAL = _____ b) TOTAL = _____

How did you score?

This quiz looks at whether you get your buzz from starting a project or finishing it off. The quiz is based on a bipolar scale with 'starting' at one end and 'finishing' at the other. The more As you score, the more you are interested in and motivated by starting things. The more Bs you score, the more you are interested in and motivated by finishing things.

You can find a full exploration of this personality pattern on page 103.

Quiz: open road or step by step?

Tick which statement – a or b – you agree with most.

1. I would choose to buy a particular new mobile phone because ...

☐ a) I was in the right shop at the right time and just happened to see one I liked.

☐ b) it matched my criteria and needs.

2. If I were showing a workmate how to do my admin and they suggested a new way, I'd feel ...

☐ a) interested – I dislike doing admin the same way every time and often vary it myself.

☐ b) somewhat thrown – I've been doing it that way for years and it's worked well for me.

3. When it comes to managing my finances ...

☐ a) I've worked out a good way of doing them, but I often find myself modifying it.

☐ b) I work them out in the same way every time; if it works, why change it?

4. If I'd just bought a DVD player, I would ...

☐ a) read the manual only when I couldn't figure out how to do something.

☐ b) read the manual carefully to find out how best to use it.

5. I prefer the kind of clothes shops where ...

☐ a) everything's mixed up and every rail is a surprise.

☐ b) everything's co-ordinated and neatly stacked.

6. At work, my brain ticks over best in an environment where I can ...

☐ a) be creative, think outside the box, allow my imagination to run riot.

☐ b) do things the right way, using tried and tested methods to get a successful result.

7. If I were assembling a simple piece of flat-packed furniture, I would ...

☐ a) start following the instructions but then find my own way to build the piece.

☐ b) follow the instructions carefully, from beginning to end.

8. When I'm getting ready to go out to work or on an evening out, I have ...

☐ a) no particular way of getting ready; I vary it from day to day.

☐ b) a set routine of showering, dressing, etc; it doesn't feel quite right if I can't follow my routine.

a) TOTAL =_____   b) TOTAL = _____

How did you score?

This quiz looks at how you tackle a task – whether you like to generate lots of alternative options for doing something or find an effective procedure and follow it. The quiz is based on a bipolar scale with 'options' at one end and 'procedures' at the other. The more As you score, the more you seek out options. The more Bs you score, the more you follow procedures.

You can find a full exploration of this personality pattern on page 112.

Quiz: jump or be pushed?

Tick which statement – a or b – you agree with most.

1. When it comes to my social life ...

☐ a) I tend to take the lead and organize what we're doing.

☐ b) my friends sort it out, while I turn up at the right place when I'm told.

2. I would feel more comfortable ...

☐ a) asking someone out on a date.

☐ b) waiting to be asked out; generally I wouldn't ask out someone I fancied.

3. I believe that ...

☐ a) I'm in control of my own destiny.

☐ b) in life, events will happen regardless of what I do.

4. If I have a problem ...

☐ a) I usually sort it myself.

☐ b) I like input from others to help me sort things out.

5. I prefer to be in a job where I ...

☐ a) make my own decisions and can act without other people's permission.

☐ b) I respond to other people's requests and needs.

6. If I was looking for a new job I'd prefer to ...

☐ a) write letters prospectively to companies I'd like to work for.

☐ b) sign up at agencies who could find me possible vacancies.

7. If I felt there was a problem in my relationship, I would ...

☐ a) speak up, even if my partner wouldn't like what I had to say.

☐ b) wait for my partner to speak up – I'd avoid rocking the boat unnecessarily.

8. If I wanted to sleep with a new partner, I ...

☐ a) would make the first move.

☐ b) would wait for them to make the first move.

a) TOTAL = _____ b) TOTAL = _____

How did you score?

This quiz looks at how much you initiate action or how much you wait before acting. The quiz is based on a bipolar scale with 'proactivity' at one end and 'reactivity' at the other. The more As you tick, the higher you score in proactivity. The more Bs you tick, the higher you score on reactivity.

You can find a full exploration of this personality pattern on page 121.

Quiz: mover-shaker or flow?

Here are two lists, A and B. For each statement score: 0 if it is nothing like you, 1 if it is sometimes like you, 2 if it is exactly like you. Then add up your total for each list.

List A

- I like to make plans and generally have order in my life. _____

- I often make 'to do' lists – but the most satisfying part is ticking off a completed task. _____

- I'm clear about my likes and dislikes. _____

- I'm aware of what needs improving in my life. _____

- I find it hard to concentrate at work if my desk is messy and cluttered. _____

List B

- Making a decision can mean I feel I'm shutting out better possibilities. _____

- I like to keep my time free and not have much planned at weekends. _____

- I often read several books at a time. _____

- If I hit a problem I take a philosophical approach and not worry. _____

- People tell me I'm easy-going, flexible and adaptable. _____

List A

- Time frames and schedules are essential for me to function well. _____

- I'm decisive to the point that having things undecided drives me crazy. _____

- If I were going on a long journey, I'd check everything before I set off. _____

- If the work targets I've set for a particular day aren't completed, I find it difficult to leave them unfinished. _____

- If my plans get disrupted I find it annoying and unsettling. _____

TOTAL = _____

List B

- 'To do' lists are handy memory-joggers, but I don't need to tick off items when they're done. _____

- If plans change at the last minute I don't freak, I just go with the flow. _____

- If I were cooking dinner, I would usually rely on my own creativity rather than following a recipe. _____

- I love being spontaneous and seizing the moment. _____

- I keep my house organized, but it might seem confusing to others. _____

TOTAL = _____

How did you score?

This quiz looks at whether you're happy to let the world go by – 'perceiving' it – or whether you intervene speedily to organize – 'judging' it. The quiz is based on a bipolar scale with 'perceiving' at one end and 'judging' at the other. The more marks you score on list A, the more you judge. The more marks you score on list B, the more you perceive.

You can find a full exploration of this personality pattern on page 128.

Quiz: higher state of consciousness

Read the following statements and circle: 3 If you strongly agree, 2 If you agree, 1 If you disagree, 0 If you strongly disagree. Then add up your total score.

	strongly disagree disagree		agree	strongly agree
• Friends and family often come to me with their problems.	0	1	2	3
• I only have to look at my partner (or someone close to me) to know there's something wrong.	0	1	2	3
• I can empathize with others when they're going through a crisis that I've also experienced myself.	0	1	2	3
• Sometimes I identify so closely with characters on the television that I find myself getting upset or angry when they do.	0	1	2	3
• I'm a great host at dinner parties as I tend to notice who needs more wine/ food etc.	0	1	2	3
• If someone close to me gets badly treated, I really pick up on their irritation or anxiety.	0	1	2	3
• If I get into a heated discussion with friends, I hardly ever go too far; I know when to keep quiet.	0	1	2	3

what makes people tick?

	strongly disagree	disagree	agree	strongly agree
• When I'm out on a first date, I pay attention to my potential mate's body language as it tells me a lot about how they feel about me.	0	1	2	3
• I'm much more interested in how humans work than I am about how 'things' work.	0	1	2	3
• It's usually quite obvious to me if someone fancies me.	0	1	2	3

Now add up your total.   TOTAL = _____

How did you score?

This quiz looks at how far you are aware of what's going on for other people, or whether you're actually more aware of what's going on for yourself.

Quite simply, your potential score is between 0 and 30 and the higher you score, the more aware you are of what's going on for other people.

You can find a full exploration of this personality pattern on page 137.

Quiz: party animal?

Here are two lists, A and B. For each statement score: 0 if it is nothing like you, 1 if it is sometimes like you, 2 if it is exactly like you. Then add up your total for each list.

List A

- I have lots of friends and acquaintances and a busy social life. _____

- I feel restless and lonely when I spend a lot of time on my own. _____

- After an exhausting day at work, my favourite way of unwinding is to go out with friends. _____

- I love being the centre of attention. _____

- People have described me as talkative, friendly, easy to get to know. _____

- I'm comfortable with meeting new people; I get a real buzz out of it. _____

List B

- I have a small group of friends whom I feel very close to. _____

- I enjoy spending time alone to reflect on my inner thoughts. _____

- After an exhausting day at work, my favourite way of unwinding is to collapse on my own in front of the telly. _____

- Being the centre of attention is my worst nightmare. _____

- I can only enjoy talking freely to someone when I feel safe with them. _____

- Sometimes I won't answer my phone because I want to be left alone. _____

- I feel drained if I spend a lot of time around people. _____

what makes people tick?

List A

- I tend to think out loud – and I've been in sticky situations for not thinking before I speak. _____

- If something is bothering me, I'll go out with friends and forget about it. _____

- I can generally talk about anything with anyone. _____

- I prefer having a chat with a friend to exchanging emails with them. _____

TOTAL = _____

List B

- I feel uncomfortable at parties, especially if I don't know anyone. _____

- Other people's opinion matters; I try not to make a fool of myself. _____

- I can seem aloof when I'm just feeling worn out by people contact. _____

TOTAL = _____

How did you score?

This quiz looks at whether you have the personality patterns of extroversion or introversion. The quiz is based on a bipolar scale with 'extroversion' at one end and 'introversion' at the other. The more marks you score on list A, the more extrovert you are. The more marks you score on list B, the more introvert. Roughly equal scores means you combine the two patterns in a third pattern called ambiversion. You can find a full exploration of this personality pattern on page 144.

Quiz: me or you?

Tick which statement – a or b – you agree with most.

1. **If I get negative feedback from my boss at work when I feel I've done a good job ...**
   - ☐ a) I'll question my boss's opinion and challenge their judgement.
   - ☐ b) I'll worry about my own capabilities to do a good job.

2. **When it comes to taking feedback ...**
   - ☐ a) I find it hard to accept someone else's opinion if it doesn't agree with my own.
   - ☐ b) I find it helps me have a better idea of how I'm getting on.

3. **If I had to make a decision on whether or not to move away to take a new job, I would ...**
   - ☐ a) come to the decision on my own, once I'd gathered all the information I needed.
   - ☐ b) seek the opinion of friends and family to help me make the right decision.

4. **I prefer the kind of work situation where ...**
   - ☐ a) I can go to my boss if I feel I need help, but otherwise I'm left to my own devices.
   - ☐ b) my boss is closely involved and gives me the praise I need to be motivated.

5. **If I were faced with temptation and resisted, it would be because ...**
   - ☐ a) it felt morally wrong.
   - ☐ b) my friends and family would strongly disapprove.

6. **If at a work function, a handful of people said I wasn't appropriately dressed, I would ...**
   - ☐ a) feel unfazed; it's hardly the end of the world.
   - ☐ b) feel self-conscious and wonder why on earth I'd chosen the outfit.

what makes people tick?

7. If I'd gained some weight which I wasn't happy about, I'd be spurred on to lose it ...

☐ a) by my own convictions.

☐ b) by the thought of how other people would rate me if I was above perfect weight.

8. If my family/friends disliked a new partner of mine, it would ...

☐ a) make no difference to me so long as I was sure my new partner was a good choice.

☐ b) bother me because I value their approval.

a) TOTAL = _____ b) TOTAL = _____

How did you score?

This quiz looks at where you take your lead from in life. Are you inspired externally from other people or internally from inside yourself? The quiz is based on a bipolar scale with 'external' at one end and 'internal' at the other. The more As you tick, the more you take your lead from inside yourself. The more Bs you tick, the more you take your lead from other people.

You can find a full exploration of this personality pattern on page 151.

Quiz: don't tell me what to do!

Read the following statements and circle: 3 if you strongly agree, 2 if you agree, 1 if you disagree, 0 if you strongly disagree. Then add up your total score

	strongly disagree	disagree	agree	strongly agree
• You tend to be suspicious of other's intentions.	0	1	2	3
• If a partner wanted you to pick them up late after a night out and it meant disrupting your plans, you would say no.	0	1	2	3
• If you and a partner argued, you'd always stand your ground.	0	1	2	3
• If your boss asked you if he could delegate your work because you were busy, you would say no; your work is your responsibility.	0	1	2	3
• You've been told you're stubborn.	0	1	2	3
• Imagine your work's cleaner has suddenly quit. Everyone's been asked to do their bit, including cleaning the toilets, but you refuse – it's not your problem.	0	1	2	3
• If you were buying a second-hand car from the local paper, you wouldn't trust the seller to give you a good deal.	0	1	2	3
• Being told what to do makes your hackles rise.	0	1	2	3
• If a friend who'd let you down several times asked for a favour, you would have to say no.	0	1	2	3

what makes people tick?

	strongly disagree	disagree	agree	strongly agree
• People 'giving you grief' makes you dig your heels in more than ever.	0	1	2	3

Now add up your total.   Total =_____

How did you score?

This quiz tests how strong-willed you are. Quite simply, your potential score is between 0 and 30 and the higher your score, the more strong-willed you are. If you score between 0 and 10 you are not very strong-willed at all, between 10 and 20 means you're moderately strong-willed or strong-willed in different contexts, between 20 and 30 means you are very strong-willed.

You can find a full exploration of this personality pattern on page 160.

Quiz: wanna be in my gang?

Here are three lists, A, B and C. For each statement score: 0 if it is nothing like you, 1 if it is sometimes like you, 2 if it is exactly like you. Then add up your total for each list.

List A

score 0, 1, or 2

- I like to work alone and be solely responsible for a project at work.   _____
- I prefer to work in an office with the door closed.   _____
- If I set myself a task to finish by the end of the day, I usually do it because I'm good at disciplining myself.   _____
- I'm fine if I have to work on my own all day – in fact I prefer it.   _____
- I find it frustrating if I have to let others participate in my work.   _____

- Delegating's difficult for me; I prefer to get the work done myself, to my own standards. _____
- Once I get my head down, I can lose all track of time because I'm so absorbed in a task. _____
- My idea of hell is when everyone tries to muscle in on what I'm doing. _____

Add up the column to find your total for list A   TOTAL =   _____

List B

- If I have to do something alone, I'm not that good at motivating myself. _____
- I much prefer working with others – they become my 'work family' while I'm in the office. _____
- I enjoy discussions that help me to understand people better. _____
- I like to be liked by my colleagues whether they're the M.D. or the canteen lady. _____
- I would never undermine someone else to further my career. _____
- I'm much more productive if a team is aiming towards a common goal. _____
- If I had to lead a team project, I'd feel uncomfortable telling people what to do. _____
- I would enjoy going on a team-building event. _____

Add up the column to find your total for list B   TOTAL =   _____

List C

- I like working as part of a team but I need to have my own area of responsibility. _____
- If I went on a team-building weekend with colleagues, I expect I'd try to manage everyone else. _____

- I do my own thing but I enjoy bouncing ideas off other people. _____

- I'm willing to assert authority if I feel it's needed. _____

- I was quite often form captain or captain of various clubs at school. _____

- If I went on holiday with a group of buddies, I'd probably end up organizing what we did each day. _____

- I find that people come to me for help when they can't get something done. _____

- I think that in a team environment, everyone needs someone to follow. _____

Add up the column to find your total for list C   TOTAL = _____

How did you score?

This quiz tests the sort of group interaction you need in order to get a job done, whether that's at work or socially. There are three patterns here:

- your score on list A rates independence; it shows how much you like to work alone
- your score on list B rates team playing; it shows how much you like to be involved with and dependent on other people
- your score on list C rates proximity; it shows how much you need to work with others yet still have your own area of responsibility.

You can find a full exploration of this personality pattern on page 167.

Quiz: my rules or yours?

Here are three lists, A, B and C. For each statement score: 0 if it is nothing like you, 1 if it is sometimes like you, 2 if it is exactly like you. Then add up your total for each list.

List A

score 0, 1, or 2
_____

- If a friend is feeling low, I'll recommend they do something that I would do to pick myself up. _____

- In a relationship, I'm clear about my views on fidelity and I wouldn't stay with someone who didn't agree with me. _____

- I will offer an opinion to friends in crisis – I tell them what I'd do if I were in their situation. _____

- I have a clear idea about my personal style and I'm attracted to others whose approach fits with mine. _____

- I stand by the motto 'do unto others as you would have them do unto you'. _____

- If I lived with someone who never did the washing up when it was their turn, it would drive me mad. _____

- I think that at work we should all stick to a similar dress code. _____

Add up the column to find your total for list A   TOTAL =   _____

List B

- Smoking is a personal choice; people should make up their own minds. _____

- It's not fair to put my views onto other people. _____

- If my partner and I had very different interests, it wouldn't bother me; we'd just work around it. _____

- If someone comes to me with a problem, I find it tricky to offer advice; everyone's different and should do what they think is best. _____
- I stand by the motto 'whatever floats your boat'. _____
- I'm often praised for my patience with others. _____
- I tend not to be judgmental of others because we all have our own path to follow. _____

Add up the column to find your total for list B   TOTAL = _____

List C

- If I were 'the new person' moving into a shared house, I'd be happy to fit in with the cleaning and shopping rotas. _____
- Whatever my partner of the time is into is fine by me; I tend to be easily influenced and adopt some of their lifestyle. _____
- I generally fit in with what everyone else wants. _____
- I stand by the motto 'so long as everyone's happy'. _____
- I form opinions on current affairs based on what 'the Media' says. _____
- If I were invited to a fancy dress party, I'd ring round first to see if everyone was dressing up before deciding whether to dress up myself. _____
- Letting others make the decisions suits me because then I don't have the worry of doing so. _____

Add up the column to find your total for list C   TOTAL = _____

How did you score?

This quiz looks at your standards and how you apply them – to yourself and to others. There are three possible patterns: 'my rules for me, my rules for you'; 'my rules for me, your rules for you'; 'your rules for you, your rules for me'.

If you scored highest on list A, then you believe 'my rules for me, my rules for you'. You have a strong sense of how you think the world should work and expect other people to think the same way and to follow suit.

If you scored highest on list B, then you believe 'my rules for me, your rules for you'. You may have a strong sense of how you think the world should work, but you are quite happy if other people don't do things your way.

If you scored highest on list C, then you believe 'your rules for you, your rules for me'. You may not have a strong sense of how things should be in the world and even if you have, you are still happy to follow other people's standards.

You can find a full exploration of this personality pattern on page 176.

Quiz: how hard do you bite back?

Here is a list of 20 statements. Tick as many as you like if you think they reflect you or your views. You should tick at least seven statements.

- ☐ 1. Conflict doesn't get you anywhere; it's much better to try to keep the peace.
- ☐ 2. If someone's going to tell me something I don't want to hear, I'll skilfully change the subject.
- ☐ 3. Conflict is healthy if it means the people involved solve a problem.
- ☐ 4. It's important that people know who's responsible for a mistake.
- ☐ 5. Catching people off-guard with a compliment is a good way to ease tension.
- ☐ 6. I've been told I can be unemotional.
- ☐ 7. I've been told that sometimes I let people take me for granted.
- ☐ 8. I can get stressed but I try not to let it affect my life too much.
- ☐ 9. Avoiding taking responsibility for my actions is a good way to shift blame.
- ☐ 10. In the past, I have taken the blame for something when it wasn't my fault.
- ☐ 11. I can keep my head clear by distancing myself when those around me are getting edgy.

what makes people tick?

☐ 12. Hopefully, people know that once a conflict with me is finished, we can then move on.

☐ 13. I'll fight my corner at all costs to make sure I can hold my head up high.

☐ 14. I dislike being shouted at, so I'll usually try to soothe the situation.

☐ 15. If I'm clever and funny enough I can keep conflict at bay.

☐ 16. If something bad happens, I cut off from my emotions; it feels safer not to let my guard down.

☐ 17. I'm not scared to confront someone – but I do it without making the other person feel bad.

☐ 18. Being over-emotional during conflict is no way to solve problems.

☐ 19. I have a long memory when it comes to remembering others who've crossed me in some way.

☐ 20. If I've forgotten to do something I said I would, some 'social flirting' keeps people off my back.

Now use the guide below to find out which conflict styles correspond to the statements you ticked.

Blaming responses 4, 9, 13, 19; Placating responses 1, 7, 10, 14; Distracting responses 2, 5, 15, 20; Computing responses 6, 11, 16, 18; Levelling responses 3, 8, 12, 17.

How did you score?

This quiz tests how you react when life gets tricky – particularly during interpersonals. There are five patterns here. Your 'blaming' score shows how far you are liable to *blame* other people when under stress. Your 'placating' score shows how far you tend to *placate* or *appease*. Your 'distracting' score shows how much you tend to *distract* yourself and other people from the problems. Your 'computing' score shows how far you tend to *cut off from* your feelings. Your 'levelling' score shows how far you tend to react *creatively* and *flexibly*.

You can find a full exploration of this personality pattern on page 185.

Resources

Anger management
- Jones, Alanna. *104 Activities That Build: Self-esteem, Teamwork, Communication, Anger Management, Self-discovery and Coping Skills*, Rec Room Publishing, 1998
- Davies, William. *Overcoming Anger and Irritability*, New York University Press, 2001

Assertiveness training
- Local evening classes often offer training in assertiveness.
- Gutmann, Joanna. *The Assertiveness Workbook*, Sheldon Press, 1998

Cognitive Behavioural Therapy
- British Association for Behavioural and Cognitive Therapists (BABCP), PO Box 9, Accrington, BB5 2GD. T: 01254 875277 F: 01254 875277 W: www.babcp.org.uk E: info@babcp.org.uk
- *How to be Happy and Fulfilled*, The Happiness Project, Elms Court, Chapel Way, Oxford, OX2 9LP. T: 01865 244414 F: 01865 248825 W: www.happiness.co.uk E: hello@happiness.co.uk
- Greenberger, Dennis and Padesky, Christine. *Mind Over Mood*, Guilford Press, 1995

Communication skills training

- Local evening classes often offer communication training and it is typically part of any basic work improvement or management training.
- Gabor, Don. *Talking with Confidence*, Sheldon Press, 1999
- Quilliam, Susan. *Body Language Secrets*, Thorsons, 1998

Co-counselling

- Co-counselling International UK Contact: John Talbot, The Laurels, Berry Hill Lane, Donnington Le Heath, Coalville, Leicestershire, LE67 2FB. T: 01530 836780 W: www.co-counselling.org

Confidence Building

- McMahon, Gladeana. *Learn To Be Your Own Life Coach*, Sheldon Press, 2001
- Roet, Brian. *The Confidence To Be Yourself*, Piatkus Books, 1999

Hypnotherapy

- British Hypnotherapy Association, 67 Upper Berkeley Street, London W1H 7DH. T: 020 7723 4443
- National Register of Hypnotherapists and Psychotherapists (NRHP), Room B, 12 Cross Street, Nelson, Lancashire, BB9 7EN. T: 01282 716839 F: 01282 698633 W: www.nrhp.co.uk E: nrhp@btconnect.com

NLP

- Association for Neuro-Linguistic Programming (ANLP), Administration Office, PO Box 10, Porthmadog, LL48 6ZB. T: 0870 870 4970 F: 0870 444 0790 W: www.anlp.org E: admin@anlp.org
- Seymour, John and O'Connor, Joseph. *Introducing Neuro Linguistic Programming*, HarperCollins, 2000

what makes people tick?